SMELL IT LIKE IT IS

Tales from the Garlic Capital of the World

Kathryn McKenzie Nichols

Drawings by Kathleen Gaschk

Fithian Press • Santa Barbara, California • 1992

To my husband, Mitch,
who only complains a little when I write about him.
Special thanks to Mike Johnson and all the people at
Nob Hill who encouraged me;
to my journalism guru, James Hayes;
to all the editors who ever took a chance on me;
and to all the people who gave me their time and tales.

—K.M.N.

The stories in this book originally appeared in the *Gilroy Dispatch.* They are reprinted here with permission of Gavilan Newpapers, Inc.

Published by FITHIAN PRESS
Post Office Box 1525
Santa Barbara, CA 93102

Library of Congress Cataloging-in-Publication Data:
Nichols, Kathryn McKenzie, 1959–
        Smell it like it is : tales from the garlic capital of the world /
Kathryn McKenzie Nichols.
            p.   cm.
        Originally published as a column in the Gilroy Dispatch.
        ISBN 1-56474-008-0 : $8.95
        1. Gilroy (Calif.)—Social life and customs—Anecdotes.
        2. Gilroy (Calif.)—Social life and customs—Humor.
        I. Title
E869.G48N53   1992
979.4'73—dc20   91-36046
                                            CIP

CONTENTS

People I've Known, Places I've Been

Modern Living: Love It or Leave It

Jes' Call Us Country Folk, Y'Hear?

Foreword

Someone much more famous than I—humorist Will Rogers—once described Gilroy as "the only town in America where you can marinate a steak by hanging it on the clothesline." This sounds like an exaggeration, but it's not too far off the mark. Gilroy processes about 90 percent of the country's garlic. In addition, the town has several tomato canneries. There are some summer days when the whole valley smells like a big pot of simmering spaghetti sauce. With extra garlic.

Some still mornings you can detect the garlic scent as far south as Aromas, 15 miles away. This is quite appropriate, since, in Spanish, it means "the smells." I live in Aromas and have worked in Gilroy since 1985, and both places are near and dear to my heart.

This area is California's last frontier for small towns. Gilroy has just topped the 30,000 mark for population, while Aromas has perhaps about 5,000 souls. I look around and realize that this area isn't going to stay small-town much longer. So I write about how things are now, what people are doing, and how life is around here. I write about those facets of modern life that drive me crazy and try to find some humor to stay sane.

I started out with a journalism degree from Cal Poly, San Luis Obispo and went rapidly downhill from there. I ended up as a reporter and editor for a variety of small newspapers in the state and living in towns so tiny that you need a magnifying glass to find them on the map. I decided it was fate and stopped fighting it. Aromas is not the least populated area in which I've ever lived, but it's close.

I wrote a weekly column for the Gilroy newspaper, *The Dispatch*, from 1987 to 1991. All the material in this book previously appeared in the column; however, it has been edited and polished slightly from its previous incarnation.

People seemed to enjoy the column, and so did I. It gave me the opportunity to record a few small slices of life in the Garlic Capital of the World and the regions nearby. I also wrote about a lot of other stuff, like the birth of my baby in 1990 and other personal matters.

I stopped working for newspapers, but I kept writing the column. Now I make my living as a newsletter editor for a chain of grocery stores called Nob Hill Foods, based in Gilroy. It's nice to still be here. I hope I'm here for a long, long time to come.

This book represents the best of my columns so far. If you don't see one of your favorites from past years, don't worry. It will probably be in the next book. Thanks for giving this a read.

K.M.N.
Aromas, California

THE GILROY LIFESTYLE:
NOTHING TO SNIFF AT

WHERE GARLIC GETS ITS START

In the receiving area of Gilroy Foods it looked like snow. Of course, since it was eighty-five degrees and August, I knew this couldn't be. The white flakes blowing in the wind were...you guessed it. Garlic.

To be more precise, garlic skin. Piling up in drifts.

In my usual disorganized fashion, I decided last week that it would be spiffy to tour the garlic processing facility at Gilroy Foods and write about it as sort of a pre-Garlic Festival column. Alas, it was not to be. The Gilroy Foods people scheduled me this week.

I'm not perfect. So sue me.

But seriously, back to my topic. I have always been curious to see the source of those delicious emanations that strike my nostrils when I drive to Gilroy each day. On occasion, I can even smell garlic in Aromas.

But dehydration production manager Tom Gallardo says that's nothing. He's smelled it as far north as Blossom Hill Road in San Jose and as far south as Salinas—both locations some twenty-five miles away. Here's a man with a nose for garlic.

I walked into the Gilroy Foods reception area, ready for my tour. Tom shook my hand and greeted me by saying, "You need a hair net." This is no criticism, mind you; it's just that everyone has to wear a hair net—men and women, employees and visitors. It's the law. This is so that you don't have to pick hairs out of your garlic powder.

Donning my designer hair net and hardhat, I felt ready for anything. Even a deluge of the stinking rose. Which is what Tom said would come my way. "Your clothes will smell like garlic for a long time," he said with a grin.

Reporting is such a strange business. You never know what you're going to smell like next.

The first stop was the receiving area, which I've already mentioned. Imagine, if you will, humongous bays stacked ten feet high with garlic. At this point, the garlic gets a vacation—four or five days of just lying around and drying out.

Tom calls this "curing." The bulbs must be dry enough so that they'll crack open easily when put into the rollers that remove the skin.

Let me pause for a few fun facts about Gilroy Foods and garlic.

Gilroy Foods has been a garlic processing facility since 1959. These days, it processes much more onion than garlic, however—Tom said about five to seven times more.

"I guess we're lucky that Gilroy didn't become the onion capital of the world," I told him.

He grinned.

Anyway, Gilroy Foods is the biggest dehydrator of onion and garlic in the industry. "It's in the multiple millions of pounds," said Tom, who noted that he can't get more specific. However, if you're interested, the next closest on the industry ladder are Roger Bros. in Turlock and Basic Vegetable in King City.

I knew if I didn't tell you, you'd be up all night wondering.

During the three-and-a-half-month garlic season (roughly July to October), the Gilroy Foods processing line goes 24 hours a day, seven days a week. About 100 people work on the garlic line, from receiving to milling.

You don't have to wonder why Gilroy smells like garlic. Just stand in the middle of the processing rooms and you'll get a good blast of odor. It reminded me of really potent garlic bread. I started salivating.

The bulbs go through the rollers and eventually all the skin comes off and the bulbs are left naked to the world. They're washed thoroughly to remove dirt. Workers are dotted here and there, but most of the work is done by machines.

When the garlic's clean, it goes into the driers—big metal ovens that heat up a room quite well. Some of the drying is controlled by computer. Through the computer, such factors as belt speeds, temperature, and product moisture are checked and adjusted.

"It's not like just sticking something in the oven," said Tom.

The dried garlic then goes into the mill, where it's chopped and ground in different ways for you, the consumer. Not only is there garlic powder and granulated garlic, there are all kinds of gradations in between.

Tom told me that not much goes to waste there—the garlic skin, for instance, is ground up for garlic powder. Some bulb material, or "meat," is ground up for powder as well.

I could go on and on about how they test the garlic for color and defects, the ratio of men to women on the processing line, etc., etc., but you get the idea. It's not mysterious. It's a big noisy place that reeks of garlic. Just people doing their jobs.

Tom leads a lot of tours through the plant. He did a good job. After I left the building, I realized that he was right: I was carrying around a definite aroma with me.

So to all of you who smelled me Tuesday and were too polite to say anything—thank you.

PUTTING A FESTIVAL IN YOUR POOL

As most everyone in southern Santa Clara County knows, the Garlic Festival is only a week away. The roads are being re-striped, the parking lot has been cleared, and window artists are decorating downtown. In ten years, the Garlic Festival has become more than an institution—it's approaching the proportions of legend.

Which is why, then, you hear a lot of interesting things concerning the festival that may not be necessarily true. You have to chalk it up to the ever-expanding festival mythology.

I am proud to say that I have tracked down just such a rumor and found it to be perfectly true. What is it, you ask? It concerns a swimming pool in Gilroy. A very unique pool. One that features the Garlic Festival logo on the bottom.

I had heard about this pool last year. I wrote down the information and promptly lost that piece of paper among all my other pieces of paper. As this year's festival approached, I began thinking about the pool once more and wondered if it really existed, or if it had been the product of a caller's fevered imagination.

I called up all the pool companies in town to see if they'd heard of such a thing. They were surprised, too. I called the Garlic Festival office. Well, they remembered giving permission to someone to use the logo in that way, but no one could remember who it was.

While I was tearing my hair out, I talked to someone who knew someone who knew someone who knew the cousin of the person who owns the pool. I talked to the cousin, who told me that the pool did, indeed, exist. So I called up Clorinda Sergi and asked if I could see her swimming pool. She didn't think it was an odd request.

When you walk into the Sergis' backyard, you can't help but notice the swimming pool. The free-form pool is fifty-one feet long. In the shallow end is a square patch of tiles painted with the Garlic Festival logo. The bottom of the pool is a dark gray-blue, but the logo blazes forth in pale yellow, clay red, and white. It's a perfect representation of the familiar trademark.

You might think that Clorinda and her husband, Jim, have some obvious link to the festival. Not really. She said they've never even worked at one, although she's been to every one of them since the event began in 1979.

When they began building their pool a couple of years ago, the Sergis were thinking of how they could make it really unique. "We wanted something weird and different," said Clorinda. She says they looked over their backyard fence and what should be there but...a field of garlic. And so the idea was born.

Of course, there is a link that goes even further back. Clorinda's father used to farm the area that is now Christmas Hill park—the site of the Garlic Festival for most of the past decade. "We used to pick prunes there when we were kids," she remembers.

She is proud of her pool and can rattle off statistics at the drop of a hat. "This is my baby," she says. It holds forty-four thousand gallons of water and contains seventy-five feet of underwater steps and benches. There is a slide. At one end is a Jacuzzi separated from the pool by a piece of custom-cut black marble. The festival logo on the pool bottom is about seven feet square.

It took them a year to build the pool, with Jim and Clorinda taking on the lion's share of the labor. But they got a lot of help from their friends. In fact, you could call the pool sort of a community project—the best man at the Sergis' wedding designed it, and Clorinda's brother designed and built the fence around it.

Yet another friend, Danny Puliafico, painted the logo. And it was he who actually obtained permission from the festival to use the registered trademark.

"It just makes the whole pool, doesn't it?" says Clorinda.

It does at that.

The pool was completed just in time for the 1987 festival. The Sergis have their own tradition of throwing a party during festival weekend, and this year will be no exception. But having people over doesn't preclude precautions. Those who can't swim are assigned "floaters." And Clorinda, who has worked as a lifeguard, is ready for any problems that should arise.

Believe it or not, the logo at the bottom of the pool does serve a useful purpose. It's positioned at the slide's splash-down point. As Clorinda points out, "When someone comes down the slide, you have to make sure no one's in the way. So you tell them to 'keep off the garlic.'"

Gilroy's Own Buffalo Stampede

One of the best things about being a columnist—or any kind of writer, for that matter—is it gives you a great excuse to be nosy. Anything that you're intrigued by is fair game for investigation. And you get paid, too. What a concept!

Such was the case with the iron buffalo by the side of the highway just south of Gilroy.

I had driven by this metal beast hundreds of times in the last few years. If you've driven down U.S. 101, you've probably seen it too. Just about every time I zipped by, I wondered: "What does it mean and how did it get there?"

Finally, after all these drive-bys, I satisfied my curiosity. I stopped. I walked to the counter of the Fruit Basket, the cherry stand adjacent to the buffalo. A pleasant-looking woman greeted me. I told her I was there to find out about the buffalo.

She looked at me in a way I have encountered often: like, "why in the world would anyone be interested in that?" She told me her son made it. And then some customers came along, and I didn't have my notebook anyway, so I wandered

15

over to look at the buffalo.

It stands on a wooden platform, nose facing 101's fumes. Its tail is a chain. The metal sculpture on its stand is about seven feet high. It is rusty from exposure to the elements.

When you get close to it, you can see how unusual it really is. It's made up of triangular pieces of metal welded together, making it look sort of Cubist. There is a metal ring in its metal nose. Someone with a sense of humor has "tied up" the buffalo with a string running from the ring to the fence.

I went back to the stand, where the woman was punching buttons on a phone. "I want you to talk to my daughter-in-law. She can tell you all about it."

So I talked to Karen Borello, who confirmed that her husband, Richard, is the artist. She suggested I talk to him when he got in that evening.

Richard sounded like he wasn't quite sure why I was interested either, but he told me about the sculpture. His family has farmed the Santa Clara Valley for three generations, first in San Jose, then Morgan Hill, and now in Gilroy. But he initially wanted to do something different with his life. He decided to study art.

He went to Chico State and went on to teach art at a little school. Then, about ten years ago, he decided he would return to the family business and came back to South County. His orchards lie across the highway from the Fruit Basket, and that's where his products are sold.

Richard embarked on the metal sculpture a couple of years ago, "when it flooded. I had a lot of free time that year." He figures he put about 200 hours into it. It is his first and last attempt at metal sculpture. "In school, I did painting, drawing, and ceramics," he said.

"I started with the idea of making a bull, but the way it turned out, it kind of made itself," said Richard, who admits that it ended up looking more like a bison.

What it's made out of seems quite appropriate for a farmer's son to use. The metal is discing blades, too worn to be useful in the fields. Richard cut the round blades into triangular pieces and welded all the triangles together.

When it was completed, he decided to put it at the family fruit stand. One problem, though: the piece weighs "probably more than a ton." They had to use a forklift.

Now it's kind of a tourist attraction. People come to the Fruit Basket, buy some cherries, look at the buffalo, and take pictures of it. "Basically, that's why I put it there," says Richard. "It's something novel."

Definitely novel. And an interesting blend of art and farming, not a combination that seems naturally compatible.

"If it ever rains like that again," mused Richard, "I might do another one."

Dry Times in California

If you're not worried about the impending drought in California, you probably should be. After all, the powers that be are going to cut into our hour-long showers and our habits of watering the lawn three times a day and washing the cat every week.

I mean, they actually want us to get it through our thick heads that water is some kind of scarce resource in this state! Can you believe that? After all, it's never scarce as long as we can haul it in from someplace else, right?

At any rate, it looks as though we'll all have to suffer through water rationing again. You may remember what it was like in 1976-77. If you don't, I have a few modest proposals to make on how to really save water. None of these brick-in-the-toilet kind of things. I'm talking ultimate conservation.

There is a lot of talk about jumping in the shower before it's hot, catching the water in a basin so you can put it on your plants, and all that. I've got a better idea. Stop bathing. Who needs it?

Remember that in centuries past, too much cleanliness was considered unhealthy. People used to boast of how little they bathed.

Just think of all the water you'd save, not to mention time and towels. After about three days without a shower, you can't possibly smell much worse. And if everyone were to smell that bad...then what difference would it make? (If you don't like it, just stock up on those five-day deodorant pads.)

If you must bathe the children, just dunk them all in the same tub. If they won't all fit, pop in as many as you can. Use the same water to wash the next set. Any child under age fifteen won't care if the water has had previous occupants.

So, you ask, what about washing the clothes and the dishes? Surely water is needed for that, you say.

Dishes are easy: just use paper plates. If you're worried about the impact of all those plates on the environment, just do what I do: erase them and use them again.

As for clothes, I think it's time California fashion designers returned to a great look of the '60s: paper clothing. Remember paper clothes? They were made out of this Handi-Wipe sort of material. It was paper, but it was tough. If your sleeve tore, all you had to do was use a little masking tape to fix it.

Back then, it was pretty much limited to paper dresses and other women's clothing. It's time to bring back that fashion and make it available to men, too. Paper pants, paper shirts, paper belts, paper hats, paper underwear—there are all kinds of possibilities. And when they get dirty or you get tired of them, simply stuff them in your barbecue and fire 'em up to get the briquets started.

Then there's the lawn problem, a great concern among homeowners in Gilroy, particularly if they've just moved in and rolled out that nice green turf about two weeks ago. It's true, a brown lawn is not as aesthetically appealing as a verdant green one. Brown lawns tend to crunch underfoot.

Nevertheless, we will have to learn to love our brown lawns.

That's why I think local merchants should sponsor a "Best Brown Lawn" contest. Prizes would go to the homes with the deadest, driest, crispiest front yards. There could also be categories for dead flowers, shrubbery and trees. However, the rules must state that the plant in question must have died from lack of water and not from unnatural causes, such as lighter fluid.

As for those pools: why not fill them with some other kind of liquid? Apple juice, for instance, or perhaps imported sparkling water. It might be a little sticky, but, hey, it'll still feel good to dive in on a hot day.

As you see, there are many ways to save water other than the ordinary. Why, we might get so good at it that we'll never need it again. Go ahead, Mother Nature, don't rain on our parade. See if we care.

ELVIS LIVES— AND HE'S BEEN SEEN IN MORGAN HILL

There has been quite a lot of interest recently in the odd and inexplicable. I have enough of that in my own life, but some people feel compelled to search for the really weird stuff.

There is a television show called "Unsolved Mysteries," for instance, which invites viewers to provide clues to particularly gory murders and kidnappings and the like. And then there are questions that come up, like "Is Jim Morrison really dead?" and "Is there a Bigfoot?" and "Do aliens really visit Earth in UFOs?" You know, all the topics so near and dear to the heart of the National Enquirer.

And then this month in Omni magazine there was a story on other unsolved mysteries. Topping the list was the case of the Lizard Man, a kind of scaly Bigfoot said to inhabit a certain South Carolina swamp. The Lizard Man is said to have three toes per foot, eerie red eyes, and a habit of sneaking up on unsuspecting motorists. Sounds like a guy I used to date.

What's interesting is that the Lizard Man is now big business in this part of South Carolina. Shops hawk Lizard Man T-shirts and so forth. Somehow, it sounds like some smart marketing guy dreamed it all up.

At any rate, at the end of the article, the editors invite readers to send in their own "Backyard Baffler," a local unsolved mystery. The winning entry will be printed in a future issue of the magazine.

I think there are plenty of mysteries to be solved right in our own back yard. I'd like to submit a few:

Case No. 1: Did Elvis visit the Burger King restaurant in Morgan Hill?

Not too long ago, a book hit the stands that got a lot of publicity. This book supposedly contained evidence that Elvis Presley faked his death and is now living in secrecy. There was a lot of talk in the media, and the author was on Phil Donahue, and all that hooey. About a month ago, someone called a radio station in San Francisco and said they'd just seen Elvis at the Morgan Hill Burger King. The talk show host, being nobody's fool, said "Thanks for calling" and hung up.

I didn't hear this exchange myself, but I called Fred Lombardi Jr., who owns the aforementioned Burger King. We had a pretty hilarious conversation about the matter.

Fred checked into it. "I asked all the managers, and no one remembers seeing Elvis," he told me. However, this story has been making the rounds in Morgan Hill, and some customers are getting a big chuckle out of it.

So who knows? If Elvis is still alive, it would be as logical for him to be in Morgan Hill as anywhere else. The King might have stepped out for a burger and fries. It could happen.

Case No. 2: How did corn and tomatoes end up growing in downtown Gilroy?

I noticed something strange last year down on the corner of Monterey and Sixth, in front of the Harvest Time Restaurant. Corn stalks were growing out of the space allowed for one of the streetside trees. The poor little tree was smothered in corn leaves.

I never did find out how the corn got there, and I didn't get around to asking anyone. I looked for the corn to reappear this year. But instead, tomato plants grew in the same spot.

You might say, "Well, it's because of the tomato trucks. They go around corners and dump part of their load on the way to the canneries. Little tomato plants spring from the seeds therein." But this is downtown Gilroy we're talking about, and I don't think big rigs are allowed downtown.

And that doesn't explain the corn, either.

Case No. 3: Why is there only one shoe beside the highway?

Now this is something I've wondered about for years. You're zooming down U.S. 101 and gazing at the median strip and all the little odds and ends that wash up there. And inevitably, you'll see a shoe. Usually, a kid's shoe. And it's always alone.

I always wonder whatever happened to the other shoe. Why is there only one? I suppose you could theorize that some mean big brother threw the shoe out of the car window. But if so, why doesn't he throw them both? Why break up the pair? Beside that, I've never seen anyone toss a shoe out the window of a moving vehicle. So why do you always see those lonely sneakers on the side of the road? Where do they come from?

You want to know my personal theory on all these strange happenings? I think the CIA is behind it all: CIA Elvis impersonators, corn planters, and shoe tossers. It's all a plot to drive us crazy.

Never Trust
a Yuppie in a
Cowboy Hat

I imagine there are a few people out there who have never heard of the Garlic Festival. I haven't yet met any, however. I remember a couple of years ago when, for some reason, a *Dispatch* reporter had to call Tokyo; the man who answered the phone, upon hearing "Gilroy," replied, "Ah, yes! Garlic!"

At any rate, perhaps you are one of the several people in the state of California who have never been introduced to the seductions of the stinking rose. Maybe you'd like to attend this year's Garlic Festival but just aren't sure how to go about doing it.

You must first arm yourself with a few things: cash, for one, and sunscreen, for another. Wearing as little clothing as possible is de rigueur (particularly for the young); it is practical as well as eye-catching, since Garlic Festival weekend invariably ends up being hotter than Hades.

You must also equip yourself with knowledge, my child, and for that you need only this column. Take your scissors, clip it out, and carry it in your back pocket for guidance when the going gets tough.

What's so scary about the Garlic Festival, you ask? Well, it has to do with the odd types of people who may attend. Here's just one spectacle to put fear into the hearts of us all:

Yuppies in cowboy hats.

You'll see what I mean once you get to the fest. Cowboy hats will be placed upon heads that have no business wearing them, heads of luxurious blow-dried hair that come from Palo Alto and places like that.

You see, these trendy-type people who invade the festival grounds only buy the hats because they think they're cute or something. They'll probably never wear them again, and they will be stuffed into the backs of closets, right next to the rowing machines and the Bart Simpson dolls. It makes one shudder to think about it. There's just something terribly insincere about this kind of person. Plus it's a waste of perfectly good hats.

But that's just one of the strange sights at the festival. You must also beware of the fellows who wear multiple beer mugs on a necklace. (Leaves their hands free to shovel down garlic-laden goodies.) The beer-mug-necklace crowd can usually be found around the grandstand, dancing maniacally to every kind of music, including New Age harpsichord tunes. After a while this type passes out on the grass, thus becoming much easier to trip over.

The festival now has a section for the kids, but those little rascals can be found darn near everywhere around the grounds. The ones you have to watch out for are those that have had their faces painted. These will try to wiggle through your knees to get a better look at something, and leave your calves a variety of interesting colors.

You must also pay heed to people making purchases at the crafts booths. Certain individuals will go crazy with the credit card and walk away with a six-foot stack of pottery. They can't see where they're going; they crash into you, and—boom— you're hit with a lawsuit claiming damages for the pottery.

Speaking of crafts, have you ever seen anyone actually buying a sweater during the Garlic Festival? There's always one artisan selling thick, beautiful sweaters, but who in their right mind would try on a sweater when it's ninety-five in the shade? It makes me sweat just to think about it.

I wouldn't trust anyone who bought sweaters, either.

But there is one very important group of weirdos to keep away from at the festival. I've never actually seen one myself, but I've heard they exist. That is…people who go to the festival but don't eat garlic!

They've got to be vampires. There's no other explanation.

A Nose for News

SHAKEN BY THE QUAKE, BUT STILL LAUGHING

Hersman Drive in Gilroy is one of those streets that you have to really look for if you want to get there. Tucked next to Uvas Creek, it's quiet and shady: the epitome of a nice neighborhood.

Things are different than they used to be on Hersman, however. Post-quake, it's a neighborhood dotted with motor homes and trash bins, fallen chimneys and cracked walls. One house has been "red-tagged"—the quake has made it uninhabitable. It's due to be torn down.

All of this made it seem rather incongruous that I would be standing inside a home on Hersman Drive laughing like crazy at a cat.

"Look at this," Polly Gariaeff said, placing the puss in question into the hole where their fireplace used to be. The cat, a large orange Persian named Flapjack, hesitated for a moment. Then he crawled up into the chimney space somewhere inside the wall.

All that could be seen of Flapjack was a tuft of tail. It shouldn't have been that funny one week after the earthquake that brought much of the Gariaeffs' worldly possessions crashing down. But we stood there and laughed until it hurt.

I had originally come over to their house to see something interesting that had happened to a ceiling fan during the quake. Polly, a good-natured soul, graciously showed me in, apologizing for the house. But the mess was understandable.

The home's two fireplaces are in pieces, as is much of the family's glassware. Framed pictures, their glass broken, lean up against the wall in one corner of the living room. Polly's husband likes to take photos, so they have a lot of these pictures. Two clocks no longer function. Inside a glass curio cabinet, ceramic sculptures of dancers have been shattered. Polly made them. "Someone offered me $150 for this one once," she said, holding up a piece of an arm. "I guess I should have taken it."

After the tour of the destruction, it seemed rather trivial to inquire after a fan.

What happened is that the cord dangling from the fan wrapped itself all around the base of the blades. The quake did it. No human hand touched that cord. It gives you the idea that the house must have literally jumped up and down.

Polly and her three children were in that room when the quake hit on Oct. 17.

Gilroy senior planner Chuck Myer told her she should save the fan, just the way it was, or at least take photos of it. It might prove interesting to seismologists. In theory, by examining the cord, someone might be able to figure out the motion of the quake. Chuck told me that a group of seismologists did come to Gilroy the other day and he wanted to take them to Polly's house. But she wasn't home, so the seismologists and the fan never met up.

The Gariaeffs even have their own earthquake album. Polly showed me the pictures of what the house looked like after it happened.

"I was canning tomatoes," she said, explaining the photo.

"The cupboards flew open and glass and spices came down into the tomatoes."

The kitchen was ankle-deep in broken glass and food. No part of the house was left unturned. "Things popped out of the closets and boxes glued themselves to the doors," she said.

It could have been worse. Their house seems to be all right. The kids are calming down. Seventeen-month-old Nicholas, perched on mom's hip, had a hard time at first, said Polly. Today he's smiling, offering me a chewed-on cracker.

Natasha, age twelve, and Sonia, age fourteen, say they're all right, although even the rumble of a truck outside makes them think an aftershock is coming. Sonia said she doesn't like the gawkers who drive up and down their street all the time just to look.

Polly's family has become famous—at least for a moment on TV—as a result of the quake. She went to the FEMA office Monday to apply for a low-interest loan, and was interviewed by Channel 46.

Polly misses the way the neighborhood was. How long will it be before it becomes its old self again? There is no telling. One change she has noticed is that she never hears the laughter of children outside, a noise that used to be common.

"It's very quiet now," she said. "Before, you'd always hear them. I heard some laughing about three days after the quake, but nothing since."

THE WAR
GOES
PRIME TIME

The other night, when there was not much on the tube except Persian Gulf news, I fell asleep in front of the TV and dreamed. But was it really a dream, or a shade of things to come?

"Welcome to the newest television extravaganza on the airwaves today—'It's Your War!' Yes, it's the latest from the war front on primetime TV! Everything you wanted to know about the death, destruction, and suffering that's taking place in the Middle East!" said a pert blonde anchorwoman.

"Tonight, we'll talk with a wounded Israeli, a paranoid American pilot, and someone who claims to know Saddam Hussein's favorite color!"

The camera zooms in on an anchorman with perfect hair. "Thanks for that overview, Shirley. Right now, we're going to take you via satellite to the front, where we hear there's a massive bombing attack under way."

The picture shifts to a desolate-looking landscape with nary a missile in the sky.

"Whoops, I guess we didn't get a good tip on that one!"

chuckles the anchorwoman. "We'll go back to that later and see if there's any action. Let's go to our correspondent in Tel Aviv!"

Shift to a man in a gas mask holding a microphone. He says, distinctly, "Hrhwogoruh. Uhgragugh!" He points at the sky.

"Thanks for that insightful analysis, Bob. We'll get back to you later," says the anchorman. "That was Bob Jones in Tel Aviv. A very interesting report, wouldn't you say, Shirley?"

"That's right, Bill," the anchorwoman smiles, showing all her teeth. "Bob, get under cover, would you? What a crazy guy. But that's a war correspondent for you!"

They chuckle again. "And now, a word from our sponsor," says the anchorman.

Stars and stripes fill the screen. "Now, Ronco presents—the only American flag you'll ever need! It's made of durable plastic, so all you'll ever have to do for maintenance is hose it off! Fly it on your flagpole! Stick it in your window! Super Glue it to the side of your truck! Show our men and women in the Middle East that you support them!

"Just send $19.99, check or money order, to Flag, P.O. Box 666, Reseta, California! Your beautiful American flag will be delivered in ten working days or less. Supplies are limited, and you wouldn't want your neighbors to think you're unpatriotic, would you?"

I tried to change the channel. No luck. "Something's wrong with the damn zapper," I muttered, and settled back into the sofa cushions to see what would happen next.

Bill and Shirley came back on the screen with big smiles. "Some exciting news!" says Bill. "We've just gotten some video tape released by the Army public information office, showing an Iraqi tank being blown up by one of our missiles!"

Something flickered weakly on the screen for a few seconds, then faded to black.

"Well, we seem to be having some difficulties with that particular piece of video," said the anchorwoman. "We'll get back to that in a minute. Right now, though, let's go to Washington D.C. to talk with Professor George Wilson. He's an expert on the Middle East and he's got some theories as to why Saddam is waging this war. Professor, can you hear me?"

On a screen behind her, there is an image of a bearded fellow in thick glasses who stares out unsmilingly. "Yes, Shirley, I can hear you," he says.

"Professor, what are your thoughts on Saddam Hussein? What's he up to, and how can he be stopped?"

"Well, Shirley, at this juncture it's not prudent to make too many predictions," said the professor. "But at this juncture I can say that Saddam Hussein is not a rational person. That much we know—at this juncture."

"Can you be a little more specific, Professor?"

"Well, he is besieged at this point. That much we know. He is under a lot of pressure—a lot of pressure. So that makes him unpredictable. That much we do know at this point."

"Thank you, Professor, for that insightful analysis," says the anchorman. "Well, that's all we've got time for. We'll see you again tomorrow night on 'It's Your War!' for all the latest developments."

Says the anchorwoman with a smile, "And now stay tuned for the hot new game show that's got all of America talking, 'Wheel of War,' with your hosts Pat Sajak and Vanna White! After that, the new comedy series 'Scuds in My Salad' will make its debut.

"Thanks for watching, Mr. and Mrs. America!"

ALL ALONE
AT THE
OUTLET CENTER

A shopping center with only one store open is a very lonely place. This was the case with Gilroy's newest attraction, the Pacific West Outlet Shopping Center, northeast of town.

If you're one of the few in Gilroy not familiar with the Outlet Center, let me back up for a moment. This center offers name-brand items at discount prices. There are similar centers around, but this seems to be the only one between Monterey and Sacramento at present.

You have to realize that the Outlet Center is the biggest thing to hit Gilroy since sliced garlic. For the first time in its history, Gilroy is on the crest of a fashion trend. Local women are abuzz about the stores there: Liz Claiborne, L'eggs and Bali, Maidenform, Hanes and more. The one problem has been that the only place open is the domain of Ms. Liz.

Let me repeat: This makes for very lonely shopping.

I went to the Outlet Center on Tuesday to check on its progress. The stores fall into four categories: open; not open but almost open; empty but with a name on the front; and empty with no name.

There is plenty of activity, though. Workmen and carpenters stroll through the immense parking lot, saying loud, masculine things like, "I'll get it in writing tomorrow," and toting various tools about. There are plenty of people hovering around the Liz Claiborne store, which opened two weeks ago at one end of the center. Most of the visitors look to be in the retiree category, with plenty of time to kill by shopping.

One older couple was checking out the unopened stores, strolling around the center as a cold wind scooted clouds across the sky. "Opening February 1," the man read out loud.

There are many pieces of paper in the windows of these establishments. Some give the opening date. Others are official-looking documents that say "City of Gilroy" and such. Still others are advertising the jobs that are coming. I was particularly intrigued by one store filled with mysterious cardboard boxes. There was no name on the store, but plenty of boxes to look at, which said things like "Made in Korea" and "Brasil—Samore." (At least I think "Samore" was the word—I was reading it upside down.)

There are other stores that appear to be just as mystifying. Forgive me for not being a proper consumer, but there are certain stores for which I have no clue what they will offer. One in particular is Harvé Bernard, which has a name on the front but nothing inside. I have never heard of Harvé Bernard. Men's clothing, maybe? Other stores are easy to figure—Toys Unlimited, for one, and Socks Galore and Leather Loft for others. At least the names spell it out for us ignorant folk.

Several stores were in the throes of preparing for their openings. By the time this column appears, they will no doubt be open and flooded with customers. These stores were a whirl of people tossing brightly-colored clothing hither and thither. Most had their doors closed, so watching the people was like looking at a silent movie. They ignored me.

There are several things I do like about this outlet center.

For one, it's tastefully decorated in shades of tan and forest green. They are nice, soothing, easy-on-the-eye colors. I also like the public restrooms, which are the only other establishments open besides Liz Claiborne.

Like any good writer, I investigated. The restrooms are also tastefully decorated, but in peach and gray. There is even a fold-down table for baby-changing. However, there were no towel dispensers. I thought this was an interesting discrepancy.

There are also machines selling Cokes and candy bars outside the restroom, as well as something called a "relaxation room." This lounge has all the charm of a prison lobby. It had only chairs and two pay telephones. It didn't look very relaxing.

The only place left to go was Liz Claiborne, which was easy to spot by the number of men hanging around outside pacing or looking uncomfortably bored.

"Do you carry maternity wear?" I asked the clerk at the front desk. "No, we don't," she replied. So much for shopping.

I wandered around anyway. There were about thirty people in the store, mostly women. I heard several discussing their color charts and how they couldn't find what they wanted in "their" colors.

There were big signs all around the store that read, "We carry leftovers, odd lots, and overruns. All sales are final." The word "final" is underlined. The signs also suggest that if you want to see the complete line of Liz, visit a major department store.

I can't really say anything bad about Liz Claiborne. I do like the clothes. The prices are pretty good, especially if you're the sort of person who thinks a sweater marked down from $120 to $84 is a good deal.

If nothing else, the window shopping is still free.

Tiny Tim
Takes a Bow

I have to admit, my intentions were not entirely good when I decided I had to go to the 30th Anniversary of Rock 'n' Roll show. It seemed like more of a curiosity than anything else, something for us '80s folks to snicker at.

The show was held at the Santa Cruz County Fair, just over the hill from Gilroy in Watsonville. We always go to this fair because it's small, familiar, and comfortable. There are nice exhibits of apples and lop-eared rabbits and cacti and farm equipment. The typical county fair.

Anyway, Tuesday was opening night for the fair, and that's when this anniversary show was scheduled. "I can't believe this," I told Mitch. "They're going to have Herman's Hermits, Otis Day and the Knights, the Coasters, and Cannibal and the Headhunters!"

Mitch grunted. He wasn't bowled over by the news.

"You know, Cannibal and the Headhunters. 'Land of a Thousand Dances.' Na, na na na na, na na na na..."

"I know how it goes," he said.

"And they're going to have Al Wilson..."

"Who?"

"And the guy who sang 'Inna-Gadda-Da-Vida' with Iron Butterfly."

"Who?"

"And Tiny Tim."

He didn't have to ask who Tiny Tim was.

We all remember Tiny Tim, even if we never saw the infamous Carson show where he married Miss Vicki on live television. It's impossible to strip from your memory the vision of the long-haired gent with the ukelele and the quavering voice who gave us his never-to-be-forgotten rendition of "Tiptoe Through The Tulips."

I had to see Tiny Tim.

So I dragged Mitch to the fair Tuesday night in hopes of catching this conglomeration of has-beens and never-weres. I didn't really think about it much until we got into the grand-stand area and started listening.

The guy on stage at that moment was Al Wilson (known for a 1974 song called "Show and Tell," and not much else). I wasn't expecting much, but he was dynamic. Resplendent in a perfectly tailored gray silk suit, he twirled and sang, danced and dipped. He was having a great time up there. His enjoyment was infectious.

The way the show went was that each former star or band got out there, performed their one or two hits, and said adios. So went the Surfaris ("Wipeout"), and Mike Pinera ("Inna-Gadda-Da-Vida").

My cynicism began to melt away in the face of these musicians, who were putting a certain amount of effort into the performance despite the fact that it was for a county fair in a podunk town they probably never heard of before. Then I started feeling sorry for them.

After all, here are these guys who have to go to a million two-bit fairs and VFW halls and school auditoriums to ply their trade. They have to take a handful of successful songs and play them over and over and over again, because that's the only way they have to earn their daily bread.

Once the show was over, they'd be back on the bus, ready to travel to the next little town on the schedule. And the next night, they'd be playing the same old songs.

Then, Tiny Tim took the stage. "Here he is," said the emcee, "the original flower child!"

He didn't look much different. Oh, a bit wider in the waist, but the hair was exactly the same as I remembered from seeing him on "Laugh-In" about a million years ago. He wore a red-and-white striped shirt and tan pants, and carried something that looked like a shopping bag onto the stage.

Tiny Tim plugged his ukelele into the amplifier and fired that baby up. Instead of "Tiptoe Through The Tulips" right off the bat, he launched into a medley of American folk songs—"This Land Is Your Land" and that kind of thing.

Then came the tulip song. He didn't sound any better than he ever did with it. But it was his only hit, so he played it.

He finished the song, and I thought that would be that. But then the emcee said, "Well, Tim, you know this is a rock 'n' roll show, and that's not exactly what you're playing."

Tiny Tim didn't take offense, but replied that he'd like to perform a song by the late great Elvis Presley. "I didn't know Mr. Presley personally, but once he wished me luck in Vegas," he noted, a trifle wistfully.

He put down the ukelele, and grabbed the microphone, and launched into "Heartbreak Hotel" in a low, gravelly voice that sounded something like Elvis on heavy cold medication. And wonder of wonders, he really belted out the song.

He finished it off by removing his shirt, revealing (gasp!) multi-colored suspenders, and then singing "I'm feeling so lonesome, I could die," and falling on the stage and kicking his feet up in the air as though his demise were imminent.

The crowd loved it.

After that, I didn't feel sorry for the musicians in the show anymore. Especially Tiny Tim. He had enough courage to go up on a stage and take his past celebrity with a grain of salt— and to poke some subtle fun at himself and the show he was in. And he was having a great old time doing it.

Having fun earning a living—that's all any of us can ask for in life.

The Things
We Do for
Lunch

"Try hitting 'enter' again," the woman behind the Carl's Jr. counter suggested as I struggled to master the machine that would pay for my meal. The tiny screen blinked up at me: AMT OK?

This was no mere tiff between me and the hunk of metal. This was serious. I had no cash, and it was up to my little ol' ATM card to get me fed. Behind me, a man waited impatiently for me to get done so that he could order a hamburger.

Ah, the things we do for lunch.

I hit "Enter" a second time on the ATM Pay Point machine. This time it worked. Salvation from hunger, courtesy of the new technology.

Carl's Jr. in Morgan Hill recently installed these Pay Point doodads, which allow you to pay for your onion rings, milkshakes, and taco salads with a bank ATM card. This is nothing new, mind you. Arco gas stations have been doing business this way for a couple of years.

The money is taken directly from your bank account and it

shows up on your next statement. The hard part is remembering to write it down in your checkbook.

You can also go into various grocery stores and use their ATM machines to buy stuff. But somehow, there's something strangely appropriate about ordering your fast food the fast way. Well, the semi-fast way, for us techno-nerds.

For the first time, you can take another medium besides money into a fast food restaurant. Before, nothing but cash would do when ordering lunch. Fast food establishments don't take checks or credit cards, so if you didn't have cash, you were stuck.

Not any more.

You can walk into just about any Northern California Carl's Jr., slide your ATM card through the machine, punch in your secret code (if you can remember it), and there you are. You can get cash back, too, if you desire. What a country!

I guess you should make sure you have enough money in your account to cover the cost of lunch, but hey, if you don't have a couple of bucks in there, you're in bad shape and probably shouldn't be eating anyway.

Assistant manager Greg Sanchez said that even he isn't carrying cash to work anymore. He just buys lunch on the machine.

"It's a big convenience for everyone," he said. Most people already know about it when they come in. Others see the machines and give them a whirl. After all, who doesn't have an ATM card these days?

Greg estimates that between twenty and thirty people use the Pay Point machines at his Carl's Jr. every day. Moneywise, that's about $150 to $200 in transactions.

Next year, the Pay Point machines are expected to go companywide. They are being tested this year in Northern California. "It's a little calmer here than it is in the Southern California market," notes Greg.

I told him I had had a delay in clearing my transaction with the machine. He said that happens. "Sometimes if you hit 'enter' before it's ready, it does that."

That was a relief. I thought it was my fault.

Greg reassured me I wasn't the only one holding up the line by figuring out how to work Pay Point. "A lot of people don't know what to do with it," he said, so the employees talk them through their first time.

Thank God it had worked for me, because I was about to fall over dead from hunger. I got my Charbroiler Chicken Club sandwich, medium fries, and a small milk, no problem. In fact, it got to my table the same time I did.

What I also found fascinating was the extremely detailed receipt I was given. Not only did it tell me what I had ordered and how much it cost, it also said in big red letters, "DEBIT TRANSACTION," giving the address, my ATM card number, the transaction fee (ten cents), the charge to my bank account, a reference number, the fact that the money came from my checking account, the date and time. Oh, and also that I did not get any cash back.

That receipt had an Orwellian "1984" written all over it. But somehow, once you're well fed, Big Brother doesn't seem to be such a big concern.

Anyway, I managed to conquer the ATM Pay Point machine, and all in one day, too. What a feeling of accomplishment! Now I'm ready for these machines wherever I may find them.

Now I just have to remember what to do with them once I get there.

ONE
WOMAN'S
COURAGE

There is a woman named Mona Johnson who is lying in a hospital bed at Stanford Medical Center, who has looked death in the eye and smiled. You might say she played poker with the Grim Reaper and bluffed him; she won back her life after all hope was lost.

I have never met Mona; I'd like to. Maybe I will someday after she gets out of the hospital. But I feel a connection. We are almost the same age. We are both mothers. And we've both been in cars struck by drivers suspected of being under the influence.

The difference is that, in the two accidents I've been in, I wasn't even scratched.

On September 14, the Jeep that Mona was driving was smashed by another vehicle, the driver of which was believed to be drunk. The impact threw her twenty feet. Like a broken doll, she lay on the pavement, life flowing out of her. Help and a helicopter arrived quickly, and she was airlifted to Stanford.

No one expected her to live. She was bleeding badly and the

lower half of her body was mangled. Her husband's aunt, Sylvia Guajardo, told me that the doctors gave Mona a variety of drugs to ease her pain, and waited for the end.

"Mona fooled them, thank God," said Sylvia, with a catch in her voice. "She fooled 'em."

But oh, at what cost. Her left leg had to be amputated. She is now undergoing a series of grafts to replace flesh that had been ripped away. She has already undergone some fifteen operations. There have been complications and infections along the way.

Her family is hoping she'll be home for Thanksgiving.

Now, you could see Mona's story as a tragedy. How sad that this had to happen. But something amazing has grown out of one woman's pain. A gathering of friends and family, the likes of which Gilroy has never seen before, has mobilized to help Mona.

They're called Friends for Mona, and they've been busy trying to pay Mona's medical bills. They've already held raffles, a bowl-a-thon, a flea market, bake sale, and car wash. There's more fund-raising to come. You can't go too far in Gilroy without seeing a Friends for Mona poster or T-shirt.

Mona's husband, Ron Diaz, is related to about half of Gilroy, it seems. And then there are their friends, who account for another major portion of the local population. Then you must also count the people who have never met Mona but have been touched by her story. "People (whom we don't know) come up to us and say, 'What can we do?'" said Sylvia.

Mona had no medical insurance. The other driver had no auto insurance. The medical bills are mounting, hour by hour. Beyond that, Sylvia said, there is another pressing need: the Jeep that was wrecked (and was impounded as evidence) was Ron and Mona's only form of transportation. He's had to borrow cars to get around.

Everyone who knows Mona will tell you what a special person she is. Her husband's cousin, Albert Valencia, de-

scribes her as a "positive influence on other people's lives....
She was always there to help other people. A real 'Mrs. Mom.'"
She is a good mother to her five daughters, Albert said—no
easy task in this day and age.

Albert and his wife renewed their wedding vows earlier this
year, and Mona did all the baking for the occasion—enough
to serve several hundred guests. This included a wedding cake,
fourteen different kinds of pies, and other sweets.

"With all the people who are helping out," Mona told
visiting family members at the hospital, "I'm going to have to
do a lot of baking when I get home."

They also invariably describe Mona as "gutsy" and "tough."
Ron's mother, Rachel Diaz, said she can't believe what a
positive attitude Mona has after all she's been through.

Rachel said Mona thinks the accident must have happened
for a reason. "Maybe to bring people together," Mona told her.
"I really, really know what it means now to have family and
friends."

Mona is not wasting too much time feeling sorry for herself,
either. Said Rachel, "She thinks of herself as lucky to be alive,
and lucky to still have one leg."

Sylvia Guajardo said Mona has been more worried about
her daughters and Ron than about herself. "She is a very
giving, very nice person. If this had happened to somebody
else, she would be right there."

Soon, the woman who wasn't expected to make it will be
giving a speech to Stanford doctors on her case. She will also
be able to celebrate her thirty-second birthday this Sunday.
And with luck, she'll be home for the holidays.

Happy birthday, Mona.

PEOPLE I'VE KNOWN, PLACES I'VE BEEN

WHERE
THE WALLS
HAVE FACES

You walk into what appears to be an ordinary wine-tasting room just off Hecker Pass Highway, no doubt hoping to sample a vintage or two. But as soon as you step inside the door, it hits you. Row upon row of famous faces, frozen in time. Celebrities past and present, living and dead.

No, this isn't The Twilight Zone. And the man standing behind the counter isn't Rod Serling. But you are about to embark on a journey through time and space. Alfred Whitaker would term it "a walk down memory lane." Whatever.

For Al, the man behind the counter at Live Oaks Winery, this mass of photographs lining the walls of the tasting room represents only the tip of the iceberg. "This is just a small sample of my collection," he'll tell you.

There are hundreds of photos, many with autographs. From Olivia de Havilland to George Bush, from Loni Anderson to Jose Canseco, from Michael J. Fox to Marilyn Monroe—the faces are all instantly recognizable.

Al claims to have one of the largest collections of celebrity photographs in the United States. He has most of it in one room of his Gilroy home. And not just photos. There are letters, clothing, and all manner of general stuff. Like a tie once owned by Dabney Coleman. Buttons from Greta Garbo's dress. A greeting card from Hitler.

Hitler?

"It's one of my most expensive items," said Al.

If you had to decide which celebrity Al resembles, it would have to be a shorter, slighter Dennis Weaver (of "McCloud" fame). A twelfth-generation American, Al has been employed at the winery for four years as "wine steward, secretary, book-keeper, dog watcher, and sales manager."

But, once upon a time, he was a photographer. That's when he began mingling with the well-known and wealthy. He personally snapped some of the portraits on the wall. He has connections that help him get others. He seeks out celebrity appearances and attends autographing sessions. And people who come into the winery often send him celebrity items after seeing his collection.

He easily recites names, habits, and backgrounds of celebrities he has known. Take Loni Anderson, for example. "She collects Snow White memorabilia and does puppetry," Al noted. "She's a natural brunette who grew up in Minnesota, and she used to be a school teacher."

Chatting with Al is better than watching "Entertainment Tonight." From him you'll also learn that the following stars are not terribly nice: Kirk Cameron, Harry Anderson, Julie Andrews, Sissy Spacek, and Alan Alda.

But there are many more nice ones. Butterfly McQueen, for instance, who, Al said, writes him regularly. Janet Leigh, Barbra Streisand, Shirley Temple Black, Joanne Kerns (who, Al points out, hails from Santa Clara). Donna Mills. Burt and Loni. Jack Lemmon. Mother Teresa.

Mother Teresa?

Al took her photo and got her autograph. "She wrote 'God bless you,' which is what you'd expect Mother Teresa to write," he said.

Most of the photos at the winery tasting room are for sale. He's parting with some of his collection because...well, it's getting to be a bit much. "It's too time-consuming," said Al. "It's tough just putting them in alphabetical order."

He does point out that he's more interested in selling wine than photos. But the display does make a good ice breaker— and inevitably, people relate their own encounters with celebs. "Someone told me recently about hiding Farrah Fawcett in their car trunk to sneak her into a drive-in in Corpus Christi, Texas."

So the next time you need a good dose of Lifestyles of the Rich and Famous-type gossip, check out the wine tasting room at Live Oaks Winery. Where, you might say, the walls have faces.

Losing Her Sight, not Her Insight

By her own admission, seventy-seven-year-old Janet Cover is old. But her philosophy is that being old shouldn't make you afraid of life.

Atop Mount Madonna, overlooking the fields of Watsonville, she writes about the tragedies that have made her strong, and the joys that keep her going.

One of life's incredible ironies is that in a place surrounded by visual splendor, Janet Cover cannot see much of it. She is going blind.

Yet it was her disability that opened the door for an untapped talent—her writing.

Here are a few excerpts from one essay, titled "On Going Blind:"

"At the moment...the prospect of total blindness is as saddening as it is frightening. When the little wild plum tree blossoms in February, the signs are pure joy. The profusion and delicacy of the flowers are a miracle of beauty. I'll have to remember my rainbows on a sunny winter day when the prisms catch and reflect the light....

"And the camellia forest. Someone can guide me down into it in the spring, but camellias aren't fragrant and I won't see the glory walking through the tunnels of camellia trees.

"Perhaps I can remember."

In another essay, she writes about what it's like to get old. She suggests that young people can gain empathy for the aged by being old for a week or so: wearing glasses smeared with Vaseline, taping their fingers with splints and using walkers.

It's odd that she writes so poignantly about old age, because she doesn't seem elderly to the people who know her. Her movements are youthful—you can see the teenager she was sixty years ago behind the glasses and white hair.

One of the people who knows her best is Luellen Reese. A year ago, Luellen became a volunteer for Homebound Seniors in Gilroy. They matched her up with Janet. And now they are close friends.

When we went up to see Janet the other day, Luellen said it's hard to tell that Janet is visually handicapped. "Just talking to her, you'd have no idea," Luellen said as her car crept through the redwoods to the little house where Janet has lived for twenty years.

It's true, Janet's bright blue eyes look right at you. She gets around well, making coffee and bringing it to visitors by herself. But tell-tale signs give her away—the oversized numbers on her pushbutton phone, the tape recorder and rack of "talking books."

She makes her own wood fire in the morning, cooks her meals, and takes care of a black cat named Oscar and a dog, Hans. Her husband died a few years ago, and she has mainly lived alone since, although a daughter, Paula, recently moved in.

Janet and her husband moved to their mountain after falling in love with it on a trip to California. They were looking for a place to spend their retirement. But their retirement was an active one: they spent more than a few years battling lumber companies who wanted to chop down the redwoods.

"We fought like mad to preserve the trees," said Janet, a cigarette held loosely in her long, elegant fingers. "It didn't work, of course."

Janet says she goes "from one thing to another." Her interests are wide-ranging. At one time, everyone who visited her was handed a lump of clay and was expected to make something with it. Janet still has the collection of objects.

"The things the men made were useful," she says with a twinkle. "The items the women made were much more fanciful."

She crocheted hats for a time, selling them at craft fairs. She was proud to be the oldest person in her creative writing class at Cabrillo College.

Then, three years ago last October, she was riding to town with her daughter when the world around her suddenly faded. The eye doctor told her nothing could be done; she had something called great cell arteritis, where overgrown cells had crushed the vein feeding her optic nerve. Nerves, once killed, don't recover. Her vision will continue to deteriorate.

Janet can see well enough to write, for now. She uses a thick black pen and writes on ruled tablets with large spaces between the lines. "How many tomorrows will there be until everything is completely black?" she writes, more in curiosity than self-pity.

"Losing your eyesight is a blow," she told me. "I couldn't do so many things that I had been doing." A counselor suggested that she write a family history as self-therapy.

"Then I kind of went off on a tangent," Janet chuckles.

Luellen describes it as Janet's "talking to herself on paper." The first time she read the essays, "I laughed. I cried. And I had this brilliant idea to do something with them."

Luellen, a motherly woman who is now volunteer coordinator for Homebound Seniors, sees Janet at least once a month to write checks for her. Now they're working to present Janet's thoughts to a wider audience.

They hope to put together a book of the essays and sell it, with proceeds going to Homebound Seniors. But they have no money with which to start, although Luellen has hopes of applying for a grant.

Whenever they find the money, the essays will be published, six months or a year down the road.

Janet admits it gives her a strange feeling to know her private thoughts will be revealed to more than a couple of people. For her, the writing itself has been enough.

"It gives me pleasure," she says. "Because of my handicap, I have to go slow. It's been a marvelous discipline."

Postscript: Janet's book was published and was well received in Gilroy. Her eyesight is no longer deteriorating, and she no longer fears total blindness. She is now a contributing writer to the editorial page of *The Dispatch.*

So How Do You Clean a Rock, Anyway?

Just another roadside attraction, as author Tom Robbins might say. That's the Rocks for you.

I go through the Rocks every day on my way to work. This is a section of U.S. 101 between Aromas and the Highway 156 turnoff to Hollister and San Juan Bautista.

Here, some long-ago engineer had to blast through and around large granite boulders to make a road. Hence the name. Heading north, it's a twisty section, a momentary rollercoaster ride that suddenly smooths out in the midst of a large eucalyptus grove.

The Rocks are a landmark of sorts. For instance, I hear that Highway Patrol officers use them as a locator for accidents and incidents. Another such marker are the silos south of Gilroy.

But I digress. Back to the Rocks. As you're traveling north, transversing the curves, you come face-to-face with a large boulder—for just a moment. Then the road dips down and away. This is a rock that gets your attention.

And there is another reason why this is no ordinary rock. It's a rock that's become a fad.

During the past two years, at least—and probably before that, for all I know—this rock has been a favorite spot for teenagers to express their opinions. In other words, it's a graffiti magnet.

I am not a big graffiti fan. Especially when there's no avoiding it. But it's been an interesting phenomenon. I first noticed it during a raging war of words between two local high schools during a basketball tournament.

Each weekend, either San Benito High School in Hollister or Alisal High in Salinas would paint the rock with highly original slogans like, "We're No. 1!" The intrepid Balers or Trojans would then inscribe their team's name.

I would always make note of the current graffiti job on Monday morning. But the funny thing was that by Tuesday or Wednesday, the rock was always scrubbed clean. And the next weekend, it would be decorated anew.

Recently, there's been some variety. After the recent Gilroy High baseball victory, guess who celebrated with a little graffiti? And this past weekend, someone with a spray can declared undying love for his girl.

So it's creativity. Who am I to knock that? It's also an endeavor that takes a certain amount of guts. There are no parking lanes or shoulders on this section of 101. There's nowhere to put yourself or your car out of harm's way. So somehow, the students have to get to one side of the road, scramble over the wall before a semi creams them, and then paint the rock. Imagine doing all this in the dark as well.

Of course, it would be wonderful if the kids were applying all this energy, creativity, and derring-do to something like violin lessons or nuclear physics. But such is the way of the world.

At any rate, I got curious about the magical disappearance of the graffiti. Like I said, after just a few days it would be completely gone. We're not talking painted over or anything.

The paint is removed from the rock's surface. I have a hard enough time getting scum off the kitchen sink. I was wondering how the heck they did it.

I called Bob Halligan, who is the district public affairs officer for Caltrans. "We've got to get the graffiti off in a hurry," he said "It gives people ideas." In other words, graffiti just breeds more graffiti.

So just about every week or two, after the paint-sprayers strike, Caltrans workers go out to the rock and put a detergent soap on it. If the paint is water-based or hasn't set, the detergent gets it off. If the paint has set, they sandblast the rock. Either way, the rock comes clean.

"We get it off as quick as we can. We can't let it stay," said Bob.

However, he acknowledged the role that graffiti seems to play in growing up. Bob waxed nostalgic for a moment about the graffiti rock of his childhood, a place called Big Rock in Marin County. But that was then, and this is now. The graffiti comes off. Quick.

Eventually, I fear, this kind of treatment would probably wear the rock down to a mere shadow of its former self. But the rock has been there at least a few thousand years, and I guess it won't get worn down that easily.

What I want to know is: how do I get these Caltrans guys to come to my house and clean my sinks the same way? After all, good help is hard to find.

THE COUNTRY STORE: CASUALTY OF PROGRESS

There is not much left at the San Martin Country Store these days. The neon-orange signs in the windows proclaim "Sale!" But this is no ordinary mark-down. At the end of the month, or when everything is sold, its doors will close for good.

Owner Ken Beatty has a pithy assessment of the store's demise: "Progress killed it," he says evenly.

This is an astonishing statement for San Martin, which still seems like the heart of the country. Once upon a time, when most of the people there made their living by farming, the Country Store was a very important place.

When it was established in 1946, it was the store with a little bit of everything. Roy Schell and Bill Agler owned it then. At first it was called Rocca's Department Store, and was part of the Rocca's Market building.

Roy and Bill got the chance to move to their own building on the corner of San Martin Avenue and Monterey Highway. It was just a garage, but the owner agreed to remodel it for them. They moved and changed the name to the San Martin

Country Store.

Chuckles Bill, "It's funny, but people actually resented the fact that we named it 'San Martin Country Store.' They told us, 'San Martin isn't going to be country forever!'"

Most small towns have a general store, a place where you can buy nails and twine and doorknobs. But the Country Store had more. "We carried shoes and ready-made women's clothing. We had a good line of women's dresses," recalls Bill. "We had cooking utensils and gifts. And of course, all the hardware and building materials."

It was a place for neighbors to gather and exchange the daily news of the town, for children to come in and buy candy. Bill ran into a young man recently who grew up in San Martin. He told Bill that when he was young, he'd save up his money all year long and go into the Country Store to buy Christmas presents.

Farmers came in frequently. They usually had to charge their purchases. "They'd say, 'I'll pay you as soon as the Sunsweet Coop pays me,'" says Bill. "That's when there were a lot of prunes grown around here."   Bill sold his share in the store to Ken Beatty in 1976. Roy sold his to his son, Pete. A few years later, Ken bought Pete's share as well.

Ken and his family kept the character of the Country Store much the same, although it hasn't carried shoes and clothing for years. But there is just about everything else you can imagine. There are greeting cards, Easter baskets, jewelry, and party hats. There are fan belts and hard hats, pipe wrenches and salmon tackle, wildflower seeds and figurines, and the miscellaneous nuts, bolts, gaskets, and screws that you need to fix that whatchamacallit at home.

Of course, things are a little mixed up at present. The once-neat aisles are stacked willy-nilly with the last few items left to be sold. "It's a mess right now," Ken says apologetically.

Ken says he'd been seeing a downturn in business long before the present recession. For the last three or four years, it's fallen off. "It's the Home Clubs and Costcos—I can't compete," he says. "Some of their prices are better than what I can get from my wholesalers."

He says he can't blame people, with times being what they are right now. The final blow was delivered by the opening of Hecker Pass Ace Hardware, which takes away a bloc of Gilroy customers who used to come to the Country Store rather than go all the way to Orchard Supply on 10th Street.

Ken—just like Bill and Roy before him—dispenses fix-it advice along with his wares. He cares about the people who come in to his store. He knows everyone, and they know him and his family. It was what you would call, in the modern vernacular, "service-oriented."

"I learned a lot by listening to other people's problems," says Ken. "I heard a lot and I solved a lot. That's the part I'm going to miss."

It seems that the Country Store's personal touch isn't much in demand anymore. People are shopping where goods are cheapest. Or perhaps they want more of a selection than a little country store can offer.

"The big guys are gobbling us up," says Ken, and he doesn't mean just his store. There are so many that have closed their doors recently—the Toy Patch and Reed Frances Hallmark and Lawtons Jewelers, just to name a few.

Ken worked at IBM before he bought the store. That was a while ago. What are his plans now? "I'm going to look for a job," he says.

Bill Agler and Roy Schell still live in San Martin. Bill is retired but active in community matters. Although he hasn't run the Country Store for a long time, it's hard for him to think of it closing.

He tells the story of a couple who came into his store Christmas Eve to buy presents. They were new in town and short of cash. They hesitantly asked if they could charge their purchases.

"We said, 'Why sure!' And do you know, whenever I saw that fellow after that, he tells me, 'I can't believe you let us do that—you didn't know us from Adam!'

"But in that business, you get to know people well. You can tell they're all right by looking at them."

THE ONLY PEACEFUL PLACE IN TOWN

Sure, there's turmoil in San Juan Bautista these days, what with recall elections and the like. But there is one peaceful place left in the mission village—the cemetery.

Actually, it's one of my favorite graveyards. This is a good time of year to go there, as long as the weather is not soggy. The old cemetery rests on a little hill, surrounded by slightly higher hills, as though you were cupped in God's hand. It is supremely peaceful.

Cemetery secretary/manager Hal Bohn enjoys the quiet as well. It's a nice place with nice views, he said. "It's great for bird-watching—a lot of migratory birds come through here."

If you're a history buff, the heart-shaped cemetery is a wealth of silent information. Two famous deceased residents are Patrick and Margaret Breen, two members of the ill-fated Donner party. They survived and became the first English-speaking settlers to live in the San Juan area.

In another section, there are nameless wooden crosses marking long-forgotten graves. Cemetery records were not kept prior to 1953, so the occupants remain forever anonymous.

The headstones give mute testimony to the harshness of life in the 1800s. Many mark the graves of children, some only days old. Often, a group of markers will have the same date of death or dates close together: the victims of some epidemic of the past.

Occasionally, a note of humor crops up in this quiet place, like the man whose tombstone is a firehouse bell. J.R. Hodgdon was his name, and he passed on in 1895. Hodgdon was a fireman, according to Hal, and after the bell became cracked, Hodgdon said he'd pay for it—providing he could use the defective bell as his grave marker.

It's one of the sights that Hal has become accustomed to pointing out—Hodgdon's grave happens to be a favorite with history classes from UC Santa Cruz. And although Hal claims not to be a historian, he is full of stories about the cemetery's past.

"In the old days, there was a Catholic and a Protestant side to the cemetery," said Hal as we walked among the headstones. "The graves of the Catholics would face south, and the Protestants would face east."

Hal, previously an art instructor at Gavilan College, has managed the cemetery for twenty years, handling everything from mowing and pruning to bookkeeping and selling plots.

He notes that the interesting composition of the cemetery attracted such notables as the late Ansel Adams, who came alone and with his photography classes.

Anyone who visits from this area will certainly see many familiar surnames engraved on the stones. There is no specific "old section" and "new section"—you just have to wander around to find what you want. As in any cemetery, there are plastic flowers galore. There were also a number of dead poinsettias on the graves when I visited, and even some leftover Christmas decorations.

The cemetery is now under the jurisdiction of San Benito County, but it started out as the church graveyard in 1838, after Don Manuel Larios donated the land to the Catholic church. Larios, the owner of a Spanish land grant, gave the acreage on the condition that his descendants could always be buried there. Hal said the Larios family is still in the area, and every so often, one is laid to rest in the cemetery.

Actually, it was San Juan's second graveyard, and so the church termed it Campo Santo Nuevo (the new cemetery). In the 1950s, the San Juan Bautista cemetery district was formed, and the county has taken care of it ever since.

Most of the older markers date from the 1860s, which marks the time when San Juan Bautista was in its glory. "It was the San Francisco or Los Angeles of its time," said Hal. "It had a larger population then than it does now."

Many of the headstones from this time are huge and ornate, carved with cherubs and flowers. Hal thinks that there were many itinerant craftsmen in the area at the time, people who had just come over from the old country and were trying to make a living any way they could. Trying to duplicate this kind of painstaking stone carving today would cost "millions of dollars," he said.

He has planted statice and poppies throughout the cemetery to bring seasonal color to the land. He also encourages families to use imagination in decorating the plots of loved ones—"I like to see them do creative things."

The older family plots are enclosed with wooden or iron fences and are scattered throughout the cemetery. There are sections for Chinese and Japanese graves, for which the stones are often inscribed with only character writing, no English.

On the way back to my car, I noticed an older woman who parked her car and walked into the center of the cemetery. She carried nothing with her. I wondered whom she had come to remember.

Riding High in a Pink Cadillac

Honey, I just wonder what you're doin' in the back of that pink Cadillac...

—*Bruce Springsteen*

That song was skipping around in my head as I climbed into the back seat of Richard Hopkins' limo. Needless to say, this is no ordinary car.

Just saying it aloud gives you a certain sort of thrill. "This is a 1959 Fleetwood Cadillac limousine," I noted to myself. "And it's pink."

"Where do you want to go?" asked Richard when he came to pick me up at The Dispatch.

"Let's cruise," I said.

The car is not a hot 'n' nasty pink, not a puke pink. It's not even a Mary Kay pink. It's kind of a tea rose pink. It sets off the chrome nicely.

There are lots of songs about pink Cadillacs. Bruce Springsteen did one. So did Aretha Franklin. There's a version of Bruce's song out now featuring Natalie Cole. But pink

Cadillacs themselves are in short supply. And as far as Hopkins can tell, this may be the only pink Cadillac limousine in existence.

"This is the year they had the biggest fins," he sighs contentedly. "In the '50s, they took fashion to extremes."

Richard, a Gilroy resident, got involved with the Cadillac about a year and a half ago. He'd been in a bad auto accident and was recuperating, but needed something to do. It just so happened he'd been looking for a '50s-era Cadillac to restore.

He found the limo, and fell in love.

At the time he bought it, it was painted black. He was mulling over what color to paint it, and was seriously thinking about white. Then his sixteen-year-old son said, "Dad, c'mon. Paint it pink."

Now the pink Cadillac is on the move, anywhere from San Francisco to Monterey. A company called Corinthian Coach in Los Gatos rents it from Richard, and that company supplies the driver.

On the road, the big engine purrs. You sink back into soft gray upholstery and put your feet up. If you want to take a few friends along, no problem. Jump seats pull out. No bar, no mini-TV here—just the basics. The back seat does come equipped with its own clock, cigarette lighters and ashtrays.

There is air conditioning, front and back. There are power windows. There's also a high-tech tape deck, into which the driver slides Natalie Cole's latest. "Pink Cadillac," naturally, is the song.

The driver, Kerry Shomura, is reminiscing. He's picked up a lot of new mothers with babies at the hospital; driven people to proms and weddings; taken it out on promotional ventures. A radio station rented it just to place the limo in different locations. If you called up and said where you saw the pink Cadillac, you'd win concert tickets.

And then there was the time he transported topless entertainment to a bachelor party. And the pink...excuse me, punk rockers who squeezed in as many friends as possible

"Most of the clientele have been extremely nice," said Kerry, dapper in formal wear and Ray-Ban sunglasses. "I never have to kick anyone out."

The car rents for fifty dollars an hour, with a three-hour minimum. Pricey, to be sure, but the car seats six, and you could split the cost. Besides, the car itself could be considered priceless—only seven hundred of the Caddy limousines were ever made.

The best part about owning this car, Richard says, is seeing how people react. "When you drive down the street, people come out of the stores yelling and screaming," he said.

Unfortunately, no one did so when I was in the car. It was only 10:00 in the morning, and downtown Gilroy was still on the sleepy side. I couldn't even find anyone to wave to.

"This car has gotten the most looks of any car I've ever owned," said Richard. "I think most people are fascinated by the '50s."

The fins, the chrome, the back tail lights are all to be marveled at. People steal the bulbous tail lights, which does not amuse Richard. Parts are next to impossible to obtain.

Richard says he's loved Cadillacs as long as he can remember. He'd like to have another '59 limo to match, but paint it baby blue. Always, the conversation returns to the huge fins, which stand a good eighteen inches high. The license plate reads, "59CADDY."

For Richard, the Cadillac is more than a car. It has aided his self-esteem, which reached a low point after his accident. He finds reaction to the limo gratifying. Not only that, but, "Everyone in town knows this car. It's a good way to meet people."

As far as he knows, there is only one other pink Cadillac for rent in the Bay Area. And it's not a limo.

"Some people get tired of regular limos. This one is really unique....If you want to be seen, you do it in this car."

Modern Living:
Love It or Leave It

VACATIONS: THE DRIVING FORCE

Going on vacation is supposed to be a joyous occasion. There you are, with all those days off work, heading for something different and exciting, such as Disneyland. So what's there to fight about?

Plenty.

I've talked to a number of people (at least three), and they've had similar experiences to my own. Vacations, particularly those taken in cars, may be hazardous to your marriage.

After extended auto treks, I'm always convinced that Mitch and I are teetering on the brink of divorce. The only time we fight is when we go on trips together. These fights are not knock-down, drag-out affairs, but the kind where you don't talk to each other for a few days. This makes it difficult to figure out details like where to stay or what to eat.

I don't know whether people with kids have this problem. You're probably so busy keeping the little ones from escaping the vehicle that you don't have time to argue with your significant other.

With us, the bone of contention has to do with who's driving and who's navigating. Neither of us wants to navigate. Both want to drive. This causes some obvious logistical problems.

The discussion in the car goes something like this, especially when we're in Southern California:

DRIVER: Now, keep an eye out for Las Pulgas Road. That's our exit.

NAVIGATOR (pointing meekly to the right): I think we just missed it.

DRIVER: Great. Just great. How are we going to get back to it?

NAVIGATOR: Don't yell at me. You should have told me earlier. It's kind of hard to peer through this smog, you know.

DRIVER: Let's try this exit.

We take the exit and wander through about two miles of back alley in some really decrepit part of Los Angeles before coming out at Las Pulgas. Then we discover it's not the road we want after all, and look for a way to get back on the freeway.

NAVIGATOR: Do you have to drive so fast?

DRIVER: This is L.A. You have to drive fast. It's a requirement of being allowed to visit.

NAVIGATOR: But this is a 25-mile-an-hour zone.

DRIVER: Hey, it's life in the fast lane.

Someone in a red Corvette passes us and flips the international symbol of discontent our way.

NAVIGATOR: (Doesn't say anything, but locks onto the armrest in a death grip.)

DRIVER: Don't make that noise when I go around corners.

NAVIGATOR: What noise?

DRIVER: Like you've sprung a leak. *SSSsssss.* And when you do that, you clutch the upholstery and step on your invisible brake.

NAVIGATOR: I do not!

DRIVER: Do too!

NAVIGATOR: Do not!

DRIVER: Wait a minute—where are we?

NAVIGATOR (looking through a vast pile of unfolded maps): Don't ask me, you're the one who used to live down here.

We pull over to the curb. Young people wearing tattoos and bandannas start ambling toward the car. Trying to act nonchalant, we pull away, burning rubber.

NAVIGATOR: Okay, take this road.

It leads to a dead end.

DRIVER: (Says nothing; just glowers.)

NAVIGATOR: So I made a little mistake! Aren't I allowed to be human?

DRIVER: Let me see the map. (Attempts to read map and steer at the same time.)

NAVIGATOR (covers eyes): Watch out for that truck!

DRIVER (in disgust): That truck is an entire three inches away. Of course I saw the truck. I'm driving, aren't I?

Very long silence descends, which lasts until at least San Diego.

I'd like to know if a lot of people have the same experience while traveling with a loved one. After all, vacation season is just around the corner. Maybe we should all get together and form a support group. We could even give it an acronym, such as Car Travel Syndrome (CTS).

Of course, we could always do something else. Like stay home.

THE TIMESHARE PRESENTATION FROM HELL

We can always tell, around our house, when summer is approaching. That's because the timeshare people start calling. And calling. And calling.

Timeshare is all the rage in vacation circles. You and fifty-one other slobs buy a week apiece in Outer Mongolia or whatever fabulous location they're pushing. Then you get to use this week every year, or trade it in for another week at some other resort that's in the network. For a small fee, of course.

This is all well and good, but these people are unbelievably persistent. They truly don't seem to realize that you don't want what they're selling. You have to scream "NO!" into the phone and then place the receiver next to the stereo and turn up that Black Sabbath album full blast.

But Mitch and I didn't know what persistence was until we endured the Timeshare Presentation from Hell.

A few weeks ago, we visited the timeshare capital of the world, South Lake Tahoe. Everyone's selling vacations, down to the little old lady who cleans your motel room. In the casinos, salespeople nab you as soon as you hit the nickel slots. "Want to enter a drawing for $20,000?" they say brightly. "All you have to do is attend a 90-minute presentation, and there's no obligation to buy anything."

They lure you in with all kinds of free stuff—dinners, gambling tokens, this and that. Okay, I'll admit it. We did it for the goodies. Which goes to prove the old saying that there's no such thing as a free lunch.

So we signed up for the 10:30 a.m. show and were ushered into a little room, tastefully color-coordinated. Some Big Chill radio station was playing softly. Coffee (free) was offered, and we filled out an exciting form that asked for the usual data and vacation preferences.

That's when we met our own personal presenter, Anne. She was an older woman with bleached hair, bad teeth, and orange lipstick. All the other couples also got their own salesperson to make the pitch.

Anne proceeded to tell us how much she loved Tahoe and how much she adored selling timeshares. She also mentioned she loved her own timeshare. "Love" was a big word in Anne's vocabulary.

She didn't love the fact that I was taking notes, however. "Ma'am?" she asked. "What are you writing down, ma'am?" I told her I wanted to take notes. "To refer back to later?" she pressed. "Yes," I said, not pointing out that's why people generally take notes.

So we got the whole pitch: why timeshare was so wonderful, the options we had in our "vacation adventures," how our share would appreciate over the years, and so forth. And then there were the fees: initiation, $250...maintenance, $300 a year...and so forth. Upgrading our accommodations cost a little something, and so did maid service, and so did changing destinations.

Anne took us on a tour of the different models of houses and emphasized how comfortable and beautiful it all was.

"Don't you just love the way they're furnished?" she enthused. We agreed it was all very nice for a place you'd only see once a year, if that.

We were led to another room to watch a video spiel that noted (again) how marvelous a thing the timeshare concept was. Then back to the first room, where Anne got down to brass tacks at last: what it would really cost. Suffice it to say it was roughly about as much as a new car, only at 17 percent interest.

Then Anne brought in the big gun: a guy in a suit who (again) told us how wonderful timeshares were, only in a slightly threatening way, like "Buy this incredible product or they'll find you at the bottom of Lake Tahoe wearing cement overshoes."

By this time, almost three hours had passed. So much for the "90-minute presentation." I started to hallucinate. Mitch started to be a smart aleck—which, for once, I appreciated. The timeshare hit man looked like he wanted to punch my husband in the nose.

"We camp out all the time, and so we travel pretty cheap," Mitch would say pseudo-innocently. "But," thundered the hit man, "motel rooms cost $60 a night, and they're going to keep going up!" Replied Mitch, "We never stay anywhere that costs $60 a night." (It's true.)

I think the final straw came when we told him our lawyer would have to look over the contract. Then, after quizzing us for five or ten more minutes, they finally let us go.

Anyway, we've decided that timeshares aren't our cup of tea. However, I think our experience would make a good plot for a horror film. The Timeshare Presentation from Hell. Coming to a resort near you.

WHEN "INFORMATION" IS NOT

I hate it when I note a disturbing trend, because it adds to my growing suspicion that the world is going nuts. At any rate, I am about to note a disturbing trend.

Time was when you'd walk into a business and there would be a friendly person to direct you to whatever or whomever you needed. Now some establishments have found out how to do away with this nicety.

I first stumbled across this phenomenon when I went to a Target store in San Jose. I had never been in this place before and wasn't quite sure what to expect. I wanted to price something I'd heard they carried, a little trailer you can pull behind a car.

The Target store turned out to be a cavernous maze, totally devoid of personality—and seemingly devoid of people. Every now and then, I'd catch a glimpse of someone in an orange vest listlessly stocking shelves. I walked among the nameless aisles, seeking some clue that might lead me to what I was looking for.

After wandering around for about fifteen minutes, I noticed a sign that said "Information." It was the only vaguely helpful thing I'd seen in the whole store. As I got close to it, I saw that an arrow pointed from the "Information" sign to a white telephone.

A smaller sign near the telephone instructed me to pick it up for directions on how to find something in the store. I picked it up, feeling pretty stupid. An operator answered.

"Hi," I said. "I'm looking for a trailer like you'd haul stuff in behind a car."

"A trailer?" she asked with doubt in her voice. "I don't think we carry anything like that. But why don't you go over and stand in the automotive aisle, and I'll send someone over to help you."

So, still feeling foolish, I took the long walk back to the auto aisle and waited. And waited. And waited. I've been in livelier mortuaries. Finally, I stuck my head into something that looked like a stock room, and said, "Hey! I need some help!"

A woman came out and told me she didn't think they carried anything like what I was looking for.

After leaving the Store of the Living Dead, I breathed a sigh of relief and chalked it up as an isolated incident. But I was proven wrong when I had the occasion to visit San Jose City Hall.

I was worried about finding city hall because I didn't know San Jose that well. So I got directions, gave myself a fifteen-minute head start, and made the trip. That part was no problem. I got there, parked right out front, and walked in ten minutes early.

The dreaded "Information" telephone was right there at the front of the lobby. I tried to ignore it. I asked a woman at the lobby desk how to find city council chambers. "I really don't know where anything is," she said. "You have to use that telephone."

With fear and trepidation, I picked up the receiver. I asked the operator how to find the city council chambers. "You go to the operator how to find the city council chambers. "You go to the sixth floor, take the elevators past the grandfather clock, and take those elevators to the sixth floor and you'll see the room," she said.

"I go to the sixth floor and take the elevator to the sixth floor?" I repeated. She gave the directions again. I argued with her. After a few minutes of this, the woman I had spoken to first pointed to a hallway past a grandfather clock where the correct elevators were.

I got to the sixth floor and found I'd been directed to the wrong room. The operator had given me directions to the offices of the city council. The secretary told me to go back down to the second floor.

In the elevator, an official-looking man got on with me. "Are you going to the city council chambers, by any chance?" I asked desperately. "I'm lost. I've never been in this place before."

"You have my sympathy," the man said. "I'll take you there."

So I finally made it to my destination, fifteen minutes after entering the building. What I want to know is this: why can't these places at least provide you with a real, physical person who can help you get to where you're going?

At least it's another good reason to stay out of San Jose.

SING A SONG
OF SPENDING

One thing they don't make like they used to is the Christmas musical. Most of the Christmas songs we know come from one movie or another. That's why I modestly propose that the Christmas musical should be revived, so at least we can get some new holiday songs. How many times can we be subjected to "Rudolph the Red-Nosed Reindeer" before we go utterly mad?

Here's my vision of the modern Christmas musical.

The scene is a typical home in a place like Gilroy or Morgan Hill, or maybe even Peoria, about 7:00 in the evening. The wife is wrapping Christmas presents before the lavishly decorated tree when the husband walks in, a glum look on his face. In the background, New Age Christmas music plays softly.

HE: Honey, we've got a problem.

SHE: What's that? You couldn't decide what to buy for your sister?

HE: I went to Kmart and they said our credit card was no good. They ran it through the machine three times, and it wasn't accepted.

SHE: The card's no good? How can it be no good? You
    mean—it got demagnetized or something?

HE: No...they said...we're maxed out. We can charge no
    more.

SHE: Maxed out? We can't be yet. I still have to buy gifts for
    all my second cousins.

They ponder the crisis for a moment as the tree lights twinkle.

HE: I just can't figure it out. What's on that card that would
    push us over the limit? After all, we had it paid off just
    last month.

SHE: Well, honey, you know how Christmas goes. There's a
    lot to buy and a lot of people to remember. All those
    little things add up after a while.

HE (suspiciously): All right, give. What exactly did you
    charge to the credit card?

SHE (looks at him with mournful eyes, and bursts into
    song):
    On the first Christmas shopping day,
    I bought my brother Bob
    a hand-held Nintendo Gameboy.

HE: But that's just one thing. Cough it up. I want to know
    about the rest.

SHE (counts on her fingers momentarily, and continues):
    On the second Christmas shopping day,
    I bought my sister Kate
    Two cordless phones
    and a hand-held Nintendo Gameboy.

HE: Come on.

SHE: *On the third Christmas shopping day,*
    I bought my Uncle Will
    three pairs of Nikes,
    two cordless phones,
    and a hand-held Nintendo Gameboy.

HE: Gotta be more than that.

SHE: *On the fourth Christmas shopping day,*

I bought my cousin Ralph
four garlic braids,
three pairs of Nikes,
two cordless phones,
and a hand-held Nintendo Gameboy.

HE: That still doesn't explain how we could max out on a
    $5,000 credit limit.

SHE: Okay, okay, here's the whole list.

Twelve dancing flowers,
eleven potpourri mini-crocks,
ten Dance Club Barbies,
nine Batman T-shirts, eight Stetson cologne sets,
seven ceramic sink stops,
six slinky sweaters,

HE: Go on.

SHE: *five...CD...players!*
four garlic braids,
three pairs of Nikes,
two cordless phones,
AND A HAND-HELD NINTENDO GAMEBOY!

(Big finish with a little tap-dancing thrown in. [Tap dancing is big
    right now, you know.])

HE: So who did you buy all those presents for, anyway?

SHE: I'm not quite sure.

HE: Say what?

SHE: I just haven't figured out who should get what. After
    all, somebody's got to like these things. They're all you
    see in the stores.

HE: We've still got a big problem, you know. How are we
    going to have Christmas without a credit card?

SHE: That's the beauty of it. We don't have to.

With a flourish, she pulls out of her purse...another credit card.

SHE: I just got this one, so we can max it out too! We'll have
    a real Christmas after all!

HE: Yes, what would Christmas be without a whole bunch of

expensive presents that we really don't need!

Here we'll have a reprise of the "Shopping Days" song, as husband and wife wave their shiny credit cards while gleefully dancing around the living room, which is already crowded with gifts.

So you expect them to pay cash or something? That's all right for real life. We're talking about the movies here.

Or are we?

MEN AND COMPUTERS: CALL THEM IRRESPONSIBLE

Computers are kind of like men, I think. You love them, you hate them, you can't live without them. Sometimes you feel like calling the whole thing off, but you always go back to them.

Only computers aren't as much fun in the kissing-and-making-up department.

I have had a love-hate relationship with computers most of my life. In school, I just missed the computer revolution. About two minutes after I graduated from college, my former journalism department was outfitted with computers.

I didn't actually lay hands on a computer until my second newspaper job. I was scared to death of it, to be honest, but I didn't have time to be nervous. There were stories to write and a newspaper to get out. So, like the Nike commercial suggests, I just did it.

Then I discovered it was quicker and easier to write on a computer than on a typewriter. Plus I didn't get that icky correcting liquid all over my fingers when I had to fix a mistake. Computers were magic.

Then I discovered why it's easy to hate a computer. Because they suck you in, you get dependent on them, and then...they break down.

Gee, this does sound more like men all the time.

All kinds of things can go wrong with a computer. A glitch in the software can send it crashing. Too much stuff and not enough memory may lead to data being lost. Even dust can snuff out your screen—not to mention what a spilled Pepsi can do.

I have lived through all kinds of computer trauma. There's nothing that gets your heart racing faster than a newspaper computer system crashing half an hour from deadline. And there's nothing more depressing than a newsroom full of blank screens and a bunch of reporters and editors anxiously doing nothing.

You'd think that would have given me the hint. But no. I finally gave in and bought a home computer, an Apple Macintosh. My brother, who works in the electronics industry, talked me into it. It was previously owned by a friend of his.

We took it home and set it up. With a flick of the mouse, my brother got it up and running. He walked me through the procedures. I grew confident. Sure, I could do this! I could be a computer-literate-type person!

That is, as long as it didn't break down.

Well, in the past four years, I've discovered that having a computer can be an expensive and time-consuming proposition. I've made all kinds of new friends who happen to fix computers. I've had the Mac into repair shops from Santa Clara to Salinas to Santa Cruz.

You see, there's one catch about owning a Mac in this area. There's no one in Gilroy or Morgan Hill who knows how to fix them.

My Mac is what could charitably be referred to as "quirky." I have other names for it when it loses my files. In most conversations, it is referred to as "the lemon."

Working on it is always an adventure. I am never quite sure what it will do on any given day. Most days, it's fine. I type, I save, I print. No problem.

Then there were days like the other day. I worked on a particular article for about two hours and then decided to create a file and save it. The Mac didn't want to save the file. Kept telling me that an error had occurred.

Patiently, I continued to try. On one of the attempts, the computer decided it had had enough, and went into a tailspin. Crash and burn.

I rebooted and was pleased to see that the file was there after all. I tried to call it up. "This file cannot be opened," read the little message. And that was that. There went two hours' work.

Of course, this doesn't even compare to the number of times that the computer has refused to recognize entire disks full of data. This is the equivalent of weeks of work down the proverbial tubes. A fairly discouraging feeling.

So you ask: "Why not get a new computer?" Because they're expensive, that's why. It just so happens that the Mac I have is five years old, which in the computer business is considered prehistoric. No one in their right mind would want to buy it unless they were going to put it in a museum. We're talking no trade-in value whatsoever.

Not only that, I doubt I could keep it running long enough to impress anyone.

The other day, when Mitch decided to use the computer for something. "How come this isn't working?" he wanted to know, referring to the external disk drive. Well, the mechanism inside had clamped down as though there were a disk in there when there wasn't. This made it impossible to put in other disks, making it about as useful as a submarine with screen doors.

Computers. You can't live with 'em, you can't live without 'em. I think I want a divorce from this one.

COMMERCIALLY YOURS

Some wit once remarked that television programs are something to take up space between commercials. Well, now TV is eliminating such useless fluff and simply running half-hour-long commercials as if they were real shows.

I have been noticing this phenomenon of late as more and more of these things turn up on the tube. Naturally, they can be found during those dead hours when not much else is on: Sunday mornings after 2:00 a.m. and early afternoons Monday through Friday.

The *TV Guide* aids and abets these shows by listing them just as though they were actual programs. A sure tip-off is the topic listed. If the show has a name like "Makeup Magic" or "Are You Desperate to Lose Weight?" it's probably just a sales pitch. Sometimes the listing simply reads "Paid Programming." Not too descriptive, but more honest.

Some shows want to sell you get-rich-quick schemes, like how to make a million with your mail-order business, or how to buy real estate for cheap. Others hawk kitchen appliances, such as the Amazing Super Wok and the Mini Blender. All those things that sound too good to be true, and are.

A typical half-hour commercial goes something like this: an ordinary-looking guy in a cheap suit appears on the screen, smiling. (They always smile when they want to sell you something.) "Hi!" he says. "My name is Joe Blow, and I want to share my money-making secrets with you! Anyone can make a mint simply by following my twenty-four-point plan for financial success! Just stay tuned."

The scene fades to a fancy-looking TV set, kind of like what you'd see on "Donahue" or the "Oprah Winfrey Show." There, Joe Blow and several other ordinary-looking Americans are discussing their financial success, which they achieved simply by following good ol' Joe's twenty-four-point plan.

And just what is this plan? Joe's smile gets even bigger as he points to a fancy-looking chart on the wall behind them. "Why, I owe it all to worm farming!" he expounds, his smile growing a millimeter longer. "Worm farming—the business of the future!"

Then Joe goes on to explain how you can do worm farming in your spare time and make mucho dinero for the price of a few crawly invertebrates and a bathtub full of dirt. And, of course, you'll need his special worm farming kit and instruction manual, which will cost just a mere $299.95. All major credit cards accepted, of course.

Then the other people on the stage explain how worm farming changed their lives, got them out of debt, enabled them to run a million-dollar business out of their very own basements, and gave them a whole new outlook on Mother Nature and how All Creatures Are Precious, Even Slimy Worms.

Of course, there is an audience. Joe Blow goes into the audience, microphone in hand (á la Donahue), and takes questions from more ordinary-looking, clean-cut, all-American folks. "Gee, Mr. Blow," goes the typical query. "How much money can I expect to make by worm farming?"

"Well, it all depends on how much time you put into it. It can supplement your present income, or you can make it your full-time job! It's completely up to you!"

At the end, an 800 number flashes on the screen, and Joe says, "If you pick up your phone and order my worm farming kit right now, you'll save $30 off the regular price! Operators are standing by!"

So naturally, we pick up the phone, and by gum, we order that worm farming kit. At least, somebody must be buying this guy's line, or these shows would have died a quick death.

The scary part is that these shows are multiplying, and not only that, a number of them have acquired celebrity spokespersons. Ali McGraw, looking and sounding like the Actress Android from Hell, plugs makeup. John Ritter, he of "Three's Company" fame, puts in his two cents for one of those financial success plans. Not worm farming, though.

You have to stop and wonder: a) how much are these people being paid to promote this stuff; and b) do they really need the money that bad? Can't they go get a cameo role in "Friday the 13th, Part 40" or something?

Of course, if the price was right, I might consider promoting a product myself. If you can't beat 'em, join 'em, as they say.

I can see my commercial going something like this:

"Are you plagued with financial problems? Love life got you down? Are you overweight, or do you want to improve your job skills? Then I've got the answer for you.

"It's the amazing Everything You Always Wanted Out of Life kit! And I'm offering it to you now at the low, low price of $489.95. In it, you'll find the answers to all your problems, whatever they may be!

"And that's not all. If you place your order today, you'll also receive the amazing Ginzu knives, with the patented Ginzu handles! Pay cash for your order and we'll throw in a copy of Richard Simmons' latest exercise video, as well as a year's supply of Cal-Ban 2000! Order now!"

JES' CALL US
COUNTRY FOLK, Y'HEAR?

WE NOW INTERRUPT THIS MARRIAGE...

Some of you out there believe that this is the end of summer. But there are others for whom the fun is just beginning.

I'm referring to that group of mostly male fanatics who are engaged in the adventure known as deer season. I should know. I married one.

Actually, deer hunting (and hunting in general) is a serious matter to those who do it. I think it's one of those male bonding things. Or it harkens back to some primeval time when you had to kill to survive. Or maybe it's just a sign of testosterone insanity.

For this guy I married, it means camping out with his father, uncle, and brother for at least a couple of weekends with nothing but Budweiser and Spam for fuel. Naturally, they choose places where the daytime temperatures will make the rocks hot enough to fry the Spam. And naturally, there's no water within fifty miles.

They run around in the brush for three or four days until all the deer have had a good laugh, and then they come home.

In the early days of our relationship, I used to worry about what we'd do if he actually brought a deer back. I knew we couldn't get it all into our incredible shrinking freezer, and it would come down to renting a meat locker somewhere for a bunch of venison that would, no doubt, sit there and wither while I figured out how to cook it.

Three years later, I don't worry so much anymore. As long as I've known him, he's never bagged a deer. Hasn't even come close.

Certain tender-hearted friends ask me questions like, "How can you stand the fact that Mitch is off murdering Bambi's father?" My reply: "Believe me, he's not."

My husband gets so excited around the whole business that he has to assemble all his gear at least a month in advance of opening day. Then, about twice a week, he goes out in the garage to rearrange it.

He takes a long grocery list with him when he runs off to buy supplies; but when he comes back from the actual trip, all that's gone are the Spam and the beer. We're stuck with 25 cans of pork 'n' beans, Spaghetti-Os, chili, and potted meat.

You know what potted meat is. It's everything judged to be too disgusting to put into hot dogs. (Of course, if I really want to get rid of this stuff, I can always accidentally drop the cans. "Oops, a dented can. Can't let this hang around!")

Of course, there's always the chance he might eat some of that stuff on subsequent hunting trips. You see, it's not over by a long shot. It is now deer season in one particular zone of the state. Another deer zone will open in October. And dove season just opened. Then there's quail, rabbit, and so on...

Of course, I shouldn't complain. I get the bed to myself for those weekends, with no one to poke in the side for snoring. When he gets back, I'm relaxed and refreshed. Inevitably, he comes back exhausted, sunburned and scratched by under-brush.

Who's the crazy person here? You be the judge.

THE ROAD
LESS
TRAVELED

Remember "Blood Alley?" Recall the dreaded stretch of Monterey Highway from Morgan Hill north to San Jose, where the thought of frequent accidents and mangled wrecks were enough to turn any driver white-knuckled?

Every commute along this stretch was accomplished in a nervous rush down the narrow corridors, past the fruit stands and traffic lights, hemmed in by those massive concrete dividers down the center of the four-lane road.

And then, two years ago, the U.S. 101 extension opened. Commuters breathed a sigh of relief, jumped into their Accords and went off to do battle in Silicon Valley.

Monterey Highway—Highway 82—was the scene of horrible car crashes prior to 1985. But it's funny how time and distance can change your perspective on a road.

I had thought of Monterey Highway as being sort of like an asphalt dragon, chewing up motorists and spitting out the pieces. Yellow flashing lights, sneaky traffic signals, and claustrophobic road space jammed with cars were the images

I kept in my mind's eye.

This all changed on a recent sunny day, when I traveled south on the highway from Capitol Expressway to Gilroy. It was the first time I had driven Blood Alley in about six years.

It's easy to forget now to take Highway 82. U.S. 101 seems so broad, smooth, and inviting. But this particular day was a Friday, around 4 p.m., and traffic was already jammed up for miles on 101.

I got off at Capitol Expressway and looked around in desperation. Some motorists' fairy godmother must have been looking out for me, because a sign magically appeared before me: "Monterey Road."

I paused just long enough to wonder why 82 is called "Road" in some places and "Street" or "Highway" in others. And then I took the ramp.

Suddenly, the traffic vanished. I was on a pleasant tree-lined roadway where no horns were honking, no tempers flaring.

I shook my head. This wasn't the Monterey Highway I remembered at all.

But then I saw the sign saying Morgan Hill and Gilroy, and knew I was on the right track. The sun shone down and I could smell flowers, not exhaust fumes. There were some cars here and there, but as I traveled south, they thinned out.

It all seemed so quaint, the remaining few produce stands and farms, the fields spread out to the west. It was lovely. I had never before been able to see past the ocean of impatient cars and my own traffic-induced paranoia.

Kind of reminded me of a poem by Robert Frost, "The Road Less Traveled."

And the funny thing is that this beauty and calm were there all the time. Sure, those darn traffic signals were still around, and the annoying flashing lights were still winking. But now they didn't bother me. Now, their purpose was clear.

Of course, it's not like it used to be. The produce stands are dying from lack of tourist traffic. The tranquility is not so conducive to business, and there is nowhere along the new part of 101 to set up a cherry stand.

But the Coyote Bait and Tackle Shop is still on Monterey Highway, and so is the Coyote Inn. And if enough folks like me rediscover the road, perhaps those places will be able to keep their doors open.

I had a bad impression of Monterey Highway and it kept me away on some subconscious level. I simply had never thought of taking the road before. And I'll bet a lot of other people don't either.

For the first time in my life, I enjoyed a ride down Blood Alley...ahem, make that Blossom Alley. And next time I head to San Jose, I'll probably go that way again.

A Vision of Chainsaws

I saw in the paper the other day where a movie company called New Line Cinema is planning another sequel to its infamous 1974 film *The Texas Chainsaw Massacre*. In case you missed it, there was a *Massacre II* that came out a few years back. Now, *Massacre III* is in the works, according to this article.

I wonder if I should invite them to film it in Aromas.

You see, living in the country means that you live in the land of chainsaws. It's a given, along with your cats bringing half-dead moles into the kitchen and roosters that crow at 3:00 a.m. The chainsaw chorus starts up just slightly later than the roosters on weekend mornings.

However, I have a slightly more intimate relationship with a particular chainsaw, which belongs to my husband. It's a fearsome weapon, especially when it's working. Mitch has a special nickname among friends who know him well. They call him "Chainsaw Master."

It all began a few years ago at Christmas. We went to my in-laws' house for the holidays, and one of the first things we did after arriving was dive into the heap of presents under the tree. One large, carefully wrapped package was addressed to Mitch.

He tore the wrappings off, and with enough glee in his voice to do credit to a toy-hungry five-year-old, he announced, "It's a chainsaw!"

I had never even been in the same room with one before.

Apparently, owning a chainsaw was the culmination of one of Mitch's boyhood dreams. It was just what he wanted. A McCulloch Eager Beaver, gas-powered, and mighty enough to chew through tree limbs at a single blow. He loved it. I could sense that I had a rival.

"Even when he was a little boy, he always wanted a McCulloch chainsaw," his mother reminisced.

Funny, most youngsters want baseball bats or fire trucks. But then again, Mitch has always been a little bit different.

Or maybe not so different. I've noticed that other men (particularly, but not exclusively, country dwellers) also have a thing for chainsaws. There must be some primal male instinct to take a noisy machine out in the back yard and use it to destroy unsuspecting plant life. I won't even mention what they're shaped like, but Dr. Freud would agree with me. Obviously, there are deep-rooted psychological implications in this whole chainsaw mania.

My husband's chainsaw lurks in the garage, feeding on oil and gasoline and working only when it feels like it. It spent two months in the shop one time, and I hoped it would never come back. Alas, it found its way home.

I don't even like touching it. It gives me the creeps, as though it were about to spring to life in my clammy hands. Maybe it escaped from a Stephen King novel. Or maybe I've been watching too many Chainsaw Massacre movies.

It doesn't help quell my fears that Mitch does a mean imitation of the main character in these gory flicks, a charming fellow named Leatherface. Leatherface swings a chainsaw over his head as though it were a lariat. Mitch thinks it's very funny to do this at home.

We also have a friend with a particularly sick sense of humor who once left the chainsaw in our living room with ketchup all over it. This was his idea of a humorous farewell. I laughed. A little.

Surely there must be a Chainsaws Anonymous group that can help poor souls such as my husband who feel compelled to own chainsaws and do strange things with them.

Of course, having a chainsaw fixation could come in handy if I could, say, get my husband a role as an extra in *Chainsaw III*. He's already got the moves down. Now all I have to do is get the producers to change the name of the movie to *The Aromas Chainsaw Massacre*.

If I could only be sure it wouldn't give Mitch any ideas...

JUST FOLLOW YOUR NOSE TO AROMAS

I live in a little town called Aromas, which is about as country as you can get. And a fact of country living is that you have animal visitors from time to time.

Some folks like this; some don't. I wish I liked it better than I do.

Everybody else, it seems, gets cute animals on their spread. They get baby fawns on the front lawn, little cottontail rabbits in the jasmine bushes, crickets chirping softly around the front door.

At least if they're eating your lettuce, they look attractive.

Our animal visitors aren't even decorative. At our house, we get the ugly, the smelly, the dangerous and the obnoxious. I'm talking wildlife revenge here.

I think our garage must have some secret little sign on it that only skunks can read. It must say, "Four-star hotel. Don't pass it up! All the garbage you can eat and lots of comfortable crevices to hide in."

I don't know how many skunks we've abruptly discovered in

the past year and a half. Open the back door of the garage, and one is likely to come scooting out. Or rummage in the garage cabinet for something, and you may start smelling that familiar odor.

Luckily, the close encounters have not yet led to any semi-permanent stenches. At least for us. The cats are another matter. They think skunk smells wonderful, and they roll in any little patch of it they can find. And then, the thoughtful little tykes, they bring it home.

There was the time a little skunk thought the dryer exhaust tube would be a perfect place to nap. Casualties: one skunk and one exhaust tube. Mitch had to bury them both in the back yard.

Drive down our road at night, and you'll probably see a skunk or two trotting amiably along in the glow of your headlights. They don't bother getting out of the car's way. Talk about confidence.

I've learned to watch my step when taking out the trash in the evening.

This is not the kind of thing that Century 21 lets you in on when selling a house. The real estate people don't bother doing a skunk count for you. Silly us, we forgot to ask.

The skunks are our most frequent guests, but there have been others that have left indelible impressions.

Take the time that I came home late one night to find a bat swooping crazily around the living room. I retreated into a stereotype. I hid in another room with the door closed and waited for my husband to come home. When he arrived, he did the manly thing and promptly chased the bat out of the house with a broom.

Then there are the lizards, which aren't terrible in themselves, but which do have the habit of turning up in the oddest places. Shoes, for instance. Under the couch. In the bathtub.

My other little woodland friends are the gophers and moles who annually make a mockery of our attempts at a garden.

Every year, I try planting things they don't like to eat. They eat them anyway. I put chicken-wire barriers at the bottom of planters; they wait until the roots grow through and then eat them.

Mitch nearly had a stroke when he watched his prize zucchini plants wiggle and then disappear into the earth. He then took to sitting in the garden for hours at a time, cradling a BB gun in his arms, waiting for the beasts to poke their noses above ground. Of course, none showed up.

We took the ultimate step and tried to gas their underground tunnels. The gophers and moles hid out for a few days and then came back to plunder anew. We briefly considered land mines, but it would be too messy. I'm now investigating planters made of reinforced concrete.

I don't even want to discuss the wasps. Or the ants.

Complain all you want to about the deer in your sweet peas. I'll trade your doe for my skunks, bats, and the rest any old time.

The Elk's Outside, Better "Hide, Hide"

I am in a sort of situation that for some reason brings to mind a dumb joke I knew as a young sprout. I think I originally read it in 101 Jokes For Children or some similarly named paperback.

Anyway, here's the joke. A teacher is telling her class about different parts of the cow. She has a picture of a cow up on the blackboard, and she is pointing out items to the class, such as hooves, horns, and so forth. She points to the outside of the cow and asks one little boy, "Jimmy, what's this part?"

Jimmy looks puzzled and replies, "I don't know."

"It's hide, Jimmy," the teacher tells him. He still looks puzzled. Says the teacher, "Hide! Hide! The cow's outside!"

Jimmy then says defiantly, "What for? I ain't afraid of an old cow!"

Thank you, thank you. And did you hear the one about the two garlic bulbs who walked into a bar, and...

Anyway, I'll tell you why this bit of foolishness is running through my tiny mind. In my case, the punchline should be,

"Hide! Hide! The elk's outside!"

Why, you ask? Am I afraid of an old elk? No. I'm afraid of this thing that's taken over our garage. It is a real, gen-u-wine elk hide from the wilds of Washington state.

It's also a long story.

My husband, the mighty hunter, has had a pretty good year. He shot a deer the opening day of the season. He's shot other various small animals as well. But the crowning glory of the year was the big elk-hunting trip in November.

That was when we went to Seattle. I stayed in the city and had a real vacation. Mitch and his brother braved rain, sleet, and snow while on the track of the wily elk. You tell me who got the best end of the deal.

I really didn't have any idea how the two hunters were doing for several days. Then I got this phone call from somewhere deep in the boonies.

"What are you doing?" I asked.

"We came into town to watch the football game and find a laundromat to dry our sleeping bags," said Mitch.

This gave me the inkling that things weren't going great.

In fact, in about two days time, they'd had every form of weather that eastern Washington has to offer. Mitch, who has become California-ized over the years, didn't take long underwear or extra socks with him. He had no feeling south of his ankles for most of the trip.

It wouldn't have been so bad, had they only bagged something. Alas, it was not to be. To add insult to injury, it seemed as though everyone around them was shooting something. The folks in the next camp over shot a 1,000-pound elk as it ran past their tents.

Well, Mitch got to know these people. After all, they had the best campfire around, and he had to dry out his socks. These people decided they didn't want the elk's hide. Guess who piped up and said, "I'll take it!"

That's right. My husband, the mighty hunter.

Dragging an elk hide around is no small thing. In fact, it's a large thing. Big enough, spread out, to cover a queen-sized bed.

So, upon returning to civilization, his first idea was to take it to a taxidermist's and trade it for something else. No dice. You see, the taxidermists all wanted to see the elk tag, which is signed by a game warden after the elk has been shot. This proves that the hunter didn't poach, but shot the poor thing legally.

However, Mitch didn't shoot the elk. The people he got the hide from had the tag, but they needed to keep it with the meat to prove they weren't poachers. No tag for Mitch's hide.

That's when he got the next brilliant idea: bring it back to our abode and tan it himself.

This is exactly what he's doing, and believe me, you don't want to do it unless you really have the urge. It's a mess.

I won't bore you with the gory details, but you have to scrape the hide and salt it and wash it and dip it in pickling solution and dry it and scrape it some more and wash it again and dry it and put tanning cream on it. Among other things.

So every evening he disappears into the garage for several hours to work on his project. It's kind of like having a rival—one that's large, wet and hairy.

Hide! Hide! The elk's outside!

If only I could.

Rewards of a Small-Town Columnist

I am not the kind of person who is good at remembering birthdays, anniversaries, or other special milestones. People who know me know this and accept it.

In fact, I recently called a friend to wish her a happy birthday—about two weeks after the fact. "Oh well," she said, "at least you got the month right."

Anyway, I bring up an anniversary of my own today: about two weeks late, as a matter of fact. You'd think I'd remember these things when they apply to myself. But no.

This month marks the second anniversary of this column. It's hard to believe that I've actually been at it this long and am still finding things to write about. That, to me, has always been the part I thought would be hardest.

Instead, I have found that there are too many people, places, ideas, and quirks worthy of Write Stuff examination. I keep a list of them on my computer at home so I won't forget about them.

Anyway, what I really wanted to write about are the odd

things that happen when you're a semi-famous person. I was not prepared for the recognition that a column would bring.

After all, I'd been the lifestyles editor at *The Dispatch* for two years before starting the column. I felt like, "Well, if people don't know who I am by now, they'll never know."

Was I ever wrong.

Now, not a week goes by that someone doesn't comment on the column. People I've never met before come up to me on the street and say, "Hey! You're that writer person! I saw your picture in the paper!"

Of course, none of my friends and relatives believe that anybody reads the column. "Oh, the column," they say. "Are you still doing that?" They aren't impressed.

Lately, I have been spotted by people in checkout lines throughout Gilroy. Usually, it happens when I'm in line at Kmart or Payless, not thinking about anything in particular besides getting through the damn line and going home.

I'm always buying mundane items like underwear and deodorant when the clerk looks up and says, "You're the one who writes that column! I read it all the time!"

It's always a shock. I never know what to say besides "Thank you very much" as I watch him or her stuff my purchases into a plastic bag. Usually it's at the end of the day and my mind is gone, and I have a hard time figuring out how to carry on the conversation.

People also will latch onto one particular column or another. I'm amazed at the number of people who remember a column I wrote years ago about my husband and his love for deer hunting. (I suspect it's taped to the refrigerators of many hunting widows.)

The other common comment is, "I read a column you wrote a few weeks ago and I just loved it." So I always politely inquire as to which column that might be. "Oh, I can't remember," they say. "But it was really good, whatever it was."

So much for deathless prose.

At any rate, to all of you who have said hello, appreciated a column or two, or written a letter, I want to say thank you. I apologize if I have seemed preoccupied when we met, but I am actually a shy person at heart and often stuck for words.

My favorite encounter of all, though, has been with a lovely gray-haired lady who came up to me and proceeded to tell me how wonderful I was, how wonderful the column was, and so on and so forth. She finished by saying emphatically, "And your picture doesn't do you justice!"

Such are the rewards of a small-town columnist.